COLONIAL AMERICAN HISTORY

THE ESSENTIAL STORY

★ ★ ★ ● ★ ★ ★

DR. ROBERT OWENS

WESTPHALIA PRESS
An imprint of Policy Studies Organization

Also from Westphalia Press

westphaliapress.org

COLONIAL AMERICAN HISTORY

THE ESSENTIAL STORY

★ ★ ★ ● ★ ★ ★

Colonial American History
The Essential Story
All Rights Reserved © 2014 by Policy Studies Organization.

Westphalia Press
An imprint of Policy Studies Organization
1527 New Hampshire Ave., NW
Washington, D.C. 20036
dgutierrezs@ipsonet.org

ISBN-13: 978-1-63391-134-5
ISBN-10: 1633911349

Cover design by Taillefer Long at Illuminated Stories:
www.illuminatedstories.com

Daniel Gutierrez-Sandoval, Executive Director
PSO and Westphalia Press

Devin Proctor, Director of Media and Publications
PSO and Westphalia Press

Updated material and comments on this edition
can be found at the Westphalia Press website:
www.westphaliapress.org

I would like to dedicate this book to the American people. Don't allow your History to be lost, forgotten or re-written. Know where you have come from so that you can know where you are. Know who you have been so that you can know who you will be.
"Those who control the present control the past
AND
Those who control the past control the future."

CONTENTS

INTRODUCTION

History has a reputation of being "BORING!" Back in the Dream Times before the dawn of the Internet, YouTube and Facebook, Early American History was almost exclusively the History of English-speaking man. The geographic area was constricted to the Atlantic coast of North America, and that was about it. Sure everyone assumed there were women around someplace, but they were merely supporting actors (or actresses as they were once quaintly called). Other European colonists, the Norse, the Spanish, the French, the Dutch, the Swedish, and the Russians were treated as minor actors waiting in the wings to be discarded as soon as it was convenient to get back to the main story about the British. The Native Americans were impediments constantly moved and moved and moved again. And of course there were African slaves but they were unfortunate victims behind the scenes of what was essentially a walk in the sunshine as the American colonies quickly rose from outposts in the wilderness to gleaming cities on a hill.

Some have called this the Imperial History. Some have called it the Accepted History. Some say it gave birth to a belief in American Exceptionalism. It had certain aspects that were almost interchangeable from author to author. The American colonists were working to improve the wilderness, to establish freedom and develop limited government, free enterprise and religious toleration. From the earliest beginnings to the culmination of the continental American empire, it was one long story of progress and victory. We never started a war, and we never lost one. It wasn't America right or wrong. It was America never wrong.

From our politically correct, highly sensitized vantage point here in the twenty-first century, it is easy to say the prior presentations of American History were simplistic, or racist, or filled with gender bias, ethnic bias, and Eurocentric. However, this critique could in itself be accused of being an exercise in Presentism, or the judgment of previous times through the distorting lens of the present. Instead we need to realize that every society must present a coherent story of why their independent and continued existence is justified and why it is important. Every society must teach their youth that there is a valid reason why their society must continue or it will soon break apart into its component parts. Multicultural societies will break apart along cultural lines, and multi-racial societies will fracture along racial lines, whatever the social tectonic plates are unless the members of that society are taught to believe in its relevance it will become irrelevant and soon cease to matter.

However, when all the actors and all their stories are added in while the History may not be as consistently uplifting or as universally consistent it is much more interesting and it is much closer to the facts. Keeping our eyes upon the past, let us begin our study seeking to present an honest, interesting, readable and brief representation of our History as we will seek guideposts that will help us navigate the future.

In this study we will work to include all the voices while at the same time expressing the uniqueness of America, its History, and its destiny.

First of all we must accept that the wilderness that has long been the stage for our understanding of European colonization in the Americas was not wilderness to the Native Americans. It was home. Many of these cultures had lived in the same areas for thousands of years. Others were newer arrivals. Whichever they were they had established nations and territories that were unmistakably developed and sovereign. They had established towns and cities many of which were permanent and extensive. They had developed some of the most important and sophisticated food crops and horticultural techniques in the world. They had extensive trade networks, worship centers, and all the other components of an advanced culture made up of varied societies.

Second, the narrative cannot exclude the less savory side if it is to be in any way complete. Therefore in our text, we will encounter the development of racially tinged philosophy, white solidarity, and the oppression and exploitation of others that became an abiding feature of English colonization. We will also watch the transplanted national rivalries that plagued European civilization wherever these Old World nations planted their flag in what was to them a New World. The text will also take notice of the fact that fifty percent of the population was excluded from political and social equality through the gender bias inherited from the past and transplanted to the colonies.

In addition, the text attempts to portray a feature of American History which is often neglected or ignored: the proposition that in the colonial period there really wasn't an "America." The boundaries which we see as firm and fixed were then nonexistent. Each colony was a separate entity and unless they were surrounded by other colonies such as Delaware or Rhode Island, they all thought of themselves as having a growing frontier in the West. They all dealt with sovereign Indian nations as well as with the colonies of other nations. The Atlantic sea lanes were an open door to the commerce and navies of the world binding America and Americans in the triangle trade between Europe, Africa, and the Americas a trade which bound together the growing community of Western civilization.

The unimaginably immense impact of the colonials upon the environment of North America is not ignored. The cross-pollination of disease, technology, flora, and fauna, and the political variations of European power strategies outline the Columbian Exchange which has had a massive influence on the subsequent development of the world. Not that pre-Columbian America was static. There had always been the same shifting patterns of life among the tribes and nations of America before the Europeans arrived, but they had always been indigenous except for the fleeting foray of the Norse. After the arrival of the later Europeans in the fifteenth century the Americas would forever be subsumed into the shifting alliances and other variables of European politics.

The larger populations of the colonists, aided by the technological, organizational and economical developments of the Europeans, possessed the power to gain an overbearing influence in the development of North America once they had established themselves along the East coast. Once the bridgehead was secure the Europeans began an almost continuous advance to the West. Using trade, alliance and war, the sphere of European power grew and grew always bringing environmental, social and political change as they displaced the native cultures. One thing that is important to remember is that the size and scope of the European movement to North America was not merely a wave or two of immigration. It was so large and so sustained that it can only be understood as migration not immigration.

This work is written for non-Historians, and is a handy easy-to-read condensed look at Early American History. It is composed of short chapters each of which is designed to be a stand-alone treatment of a segment of time. It is my hope that this book will help fill the void that is exposed by the general lack of historical perspective which I believe is a major contributor to America's current lack of self-awareness of and appreciation for the uniqueness which is the United States.

-Robert R. Owens

INDIANS

Native Americans (even pre-Columbian ones) are often enlisted in our contemporary debates through commercials and quotes, such as when Iron Eyes Cody an Italian-American actor famous for portraying Indians stood with an artificial tear rolling down his cheek as he looked at discarded fast food wrappers, or, the stirring environmental speech supposedly given by Chief Seattle which has no basis in History. This is the attempted manipulation of modern populations through the exploitation and distortion of another culture. It is cultural chauvinism of the most blatant kind and shows no respect or appreciation for the dignity of others. Our study seeks to avoid this type of crass insensitivity and to discuss the culture which makes up the milieu of American colonial life in context.

Where did the Native Americans come from? Most experts propose and support the Land Bridge or Bearing Straight Theory. This theory, which is rejected by most Native Americans, posits that during the last ice age the water levels fell so low that the Bearing Straight between North America and Asia became dry land. Across this land bridge the ancestors of the Native Americans, tribal people from Siberia and Mongolia, crossed spreading out to fill both North and South America. Native Americans point to their own histories and cultural knowledge to dispute these theories most attesting to the belief that they were always here. However some variation of the immigration theories is generally accepted by non-Native American scholars.

According to the migration theories the initial and the largest waves of migration ended approximately 10,000 years ago as the retreating glaciers brought sea levels to their modern levels. Subsequent waves of migration were accomplished by tribes with boats such as the Intuits and

Aleuts. These Paleo-Indians lived by hunting and gathering as was typical of all Paleolithic peoples. They followed herds and weather patterns seeking better living conditions and adequate food supplies ever spreading out South and East to fill every nook and cranny of the Americas. These resourceful people adapted to the many different environmental niches building societies and technologies that utilized available resources to an amazing degree.

The occupation of the land soon wrought changes. The large mammals such as the giant beaver, the mastodon, the horse and the camel which once covered the vast grasslands died out or were hunted to extinction. The climate warmed and the circumstances changed. Growing populations began to jostle for resources and constant subdivision soon brought contending groups to a land once devoid of humanity.

As time progressed, the Paleo-Indians of the early migration period developed into the Archaic Indians of tribal history. These people became adept at horticulture changing and adapting the landscape to meet their needs. The increase of food supplies combined with the warming climate led to increased life spans, population growth and further solidification of cultural differences. The ingenuity and skill of the various Native American peoples in adapting wild plants to their use is seen in the many crops which through the Columbian Exchange have become staples of the world's food supply.

Many large and highly specialized cultures developed in the area that would one day become the United States.

In the Southwest the Anasazi and the Hohokam built great cities and some of the largest irrigation systems in the ancient world. They established trading networks that stretched across the continent and deep into Central America. These remarkable people built impressive cliff dwellings and the vast complexes such as in Chaco Canyon and Mesa Verde. These cultures also developed pottery and horticulture to an amazing degree. Their distinctive pottery motifs are still popular and the large surpluses of food they were able to grow supported a diverse and specialized civilization that endured for hundreds and perhaps thousands of years.

The Mound Builders built impressive cities and controlled a large area along the Mississippi and Ohio rivers. They built their cities as far North as Minnesota and as far South as Florida, as far west as Oklahoma and as far East as Ohio. They built the great city of Cahokia in what is today Illinois. At its peak Cahokia was the largest settlement north of central Mexico. It thrived for more than three centuries. This city of pyramids and paved streets possessed a population from 10,000 to 20,000. They erected the third largest pyramid in the Americas. The traders from Cahokia traveled across much of North America, from the Gulf Coast to the Great Lakes, from the Atlantic coast to Oklahoma.

The Native Americans had many different religious beliefs. Overall these religious systems can almost universally be typified as animism. Which is a belief in numerous personalized, supernatural beings endowed with reason, intelligence and volition. And that these beings inhabit both objects and living beings and govern their existences. Basically this is the belief that everything is conscious, and that everything has a soul. The term has been further extended to refer to a belief that the natural world is a community of living personas, only some of whom are human.

Important parts of these beliefs included respect for all things believed to have a spirit, the use of dreams and visions as a means to communicate with the spirit world and shamanism. Once the Europeans arrived their various versions of Christianity intruded into the religious beliefs and practices of the Native Americans. This often led to a blend of the two religious systems best typified by the development and growth of the Native American Church.

These are the people who greeted the Europeans as they arrived in the Americas. They were a highly social people divided into multiple civilizations and cultures. Their technology was as varied as their languages and their societies ranged from simple to highly complex. One thing they weren't was savages in an untamed wilderness.

★

CONQUISTADORS

Several factors converged to create the climate for European dominance after the fifteenth century.

The growing populations and limited resources provided a social impetus for expansion. The accumulation of wealth and a mercantilist economic policy which sought to make every country self-sufficient drove the Europeans to seek both raw materials and markets which could be appropriated as possessions. The development of technology in the spheres of ocean-going ships and weapons provided the transport to far-off places and the ability to overcome the primitive weapons of what were almost always the superior numbers of the indigenous peoples. A tradition of crusades especially the Iberian Reconquista and a feeling of cultural superiority combined with a religion based on evangelism provided a philosophical rationale for overseas conquest. In addition organizational skills and techniques in government, military and business provided the means to mobilize the forces necessary to confront and overcome much larger populations and the ability to impose their various colonial establishments.

A geo-political motive also had a significant interplay in the European drive for exploration. The Islamic powers controlled the trade routes between sub-Saharan Africa and East Asia. The leaders of Europe saw their wealth being drained away to pay for the trade goods desired by their populations. It was the desire to find alternative trade routes that provided the initial impetus for exploration of the Atlantic sea routes.

The Iberian Peninsula which had been under Islamic domination for hundreds of years fought a century-long series of wars to dislodge the invaders. Finally in 1492 the combined might of the kingdoms of Aragon, Castile and Portugal finally triumphed and expelled the Moors. They immediately confronted a new problem, what to do with the thousands of unemployed crusaders. These hardened troops were used to nothing but war. They were skilled in nothing but fighting. Suddenly instead of being the most necessary of citizens they became a burden upon the treasury and an impediment to the growth of civil society.

With a coast and ports facing the West and South both Spain and Portugal took the lead in exploring the Atlantic. They established colonies in the Canary Islands, Madeiras, and the Azores which became convenient jumping-off points for ever further ventures into the unknown. Once new lands were found, the Kingdoms poured in legions of veteran troops to subdue and take possession.

At first the Iberians led by Portugal sought for a way around Africa. Incrementally, year after year they went further and further south. Once they had established their outposts in the Canary Islands they soon began the more intense project of colonization. The native populations were overwhelmed and replaced. Then as the riches in fish and forest products flowed to the homelands the safe harbors provided bases for the continued probes along the African coast.

Finally in 1487 the Portuguese mariner Bartolomeu Dias rounded the southern tip of Africa and in 1498 Vasco da Gama followed Dias' trail and crossed the Indian Ocean completing the European's long search of an alternative route to the riches of the East. This put Portugal in the forefront as a colonizing and trading power. But this success and concentration on their now lucrative trade route to the south and east also diverted their attention from heading west. Seeing the riches and prestige that Portugal was gaining from their new empire Spain, excluded from the way south by Portugal's success and power turned west.

The way west was not new. For hundreds of years the people of the North, Norway, Denmark and Sweden had traveled to the Faores, Iceland and Greenland. In approximately the year 1000 the Norse moved on from their island bases to actually reach the northeaster edge of North America making landfalls on Baffin Island, Labrador and Newfoundland. In a place they called Vinland they established the first European colony in North America. This colony lasted no more than a generation before succumbing to a lack of support and hostility with the Native Americans.

Columbus, an Italian, was an experienced mariner who had trained under the Portuguese. He had lived and worked for the Portuguese for many years but when they refused to finance his quest for a route to the East across the Atlantic he turned to Spain.

Although it is a well-accepted legend that everyone thought the world was flat and that Columbus had to battle against the ignorance of the Spanish leaders to get financing this is not true. It was a generally accepted fact among the European intellectuals of the day that the world was round. This knowledge had been discovered by the ancient Greeks. The leaders of Spain didn't fear sending ships to fall off the end of the earth they simply believed that the distance was so far no one could carry enough supplies to make the voyage. Their miscalculation was not in the shape of the planet or the size of the ocean instead their problem was that they didn't imagine that other continents might bar the way.

The reason for Columbus' belief that he could successfully sail from Europe to the East was that he miscalculated the distance. His mistake gave him the confidence to head west to arrive in the East. This confidence eventually led the monarchs of Spain to invest a small fleet of three ships in what would prove to be one of the best investments of all time.

When Columbus arrived in the Caribbean he encountered the Taino people who were technologically and organizationally primitive compared to the Spanish. Immediately Columbus began to replicate the colonization and subjugation process which had proven so effective in the Canary

Islands. And then another new European invention made as big an impact on the Americas as the firearms and ships. The printing press quickly spread the word of the discovery and soon every European country began preparing to join the drive to the west in any way they could.

The Spanish were eager to expand and exploit their discovery. In less than a year Columbus returned with 17 ships and more than 1,000 men. The first farmers and artisans began remaking the islands into the colonial environment which was to become all too familiar. The introduction of slavery and disease soon decimated the native populations as the Spanish transformed the New World into an approximation of the Old World while the increase in the European food supply spurred by the introduction of American crops such as corn and potatoes increased the supply of potential colonists. When we combine all this with the detrimental impacts of the Columbian Exchange such as the introduction of pigs which soon became voracious wild animals destroying Native crops the New World as an Eden ended as the Old World invaded.

★

THE SPANISH EMPIRE

The sixteenth century saw the rise of the world-girdling Spanish Empire larger and more diverse than even the Roman Empire at its zenith the Spanish Empire dominated the power politics of Europe. The steady stream of unemployed warriors Spain had to export conquered empires larger and richer than Spain itself in the Aztecs and the Inca. The plunder and wealth of the Americas fueled a lavish political and military agenda not to mention an imperial life-style for the proud Spaniards.

The other maritime nations of Europe attempted as best as they could to emulate the Spanish. They struggled to found colonies in the cooler climes where the Natives encountered did not offer as immediate a benefit as easy a conquest or as abundant plunder. War after war convulsed Europe and their various empires as they all jockeyed for power and influence.

The Spanish faced many challenges as their empire grew. They had to deal with the rise of the Conquistadors. These men were independent contractors not government agents. Once they had established themselves as the new apex of the American pyramids they sought to rule as semi-autonomous war-lords but the Imperial government back in Spain would have none of it. Soon charges were brought against the most blatantly rebellious and the rest were brought into line. Spain meant to have an efficient colonial regime that delivered the optimum amount of wealth to Europe for the advancement of the mother country.

One thing that got in the way of this plan was the constant attacks of pirates and freebooters from other European countries. They preyed upon the treasure fleets and sacked coastal towns until Spain had to begin spending vast amounts of money for fortifications. These eventually became some of the greatest fortresses in the world and cost so much money that the flow of treasure home was seriously curtailed.

As time went on the other European powers began to see that while piracy could win immense profits it couldn't supply a steady income. In consequence, the drive to establish competing colonies was strengthened. Eventually Spain, which claimed all of North America, was face to face with strong and growing colonies planted by both England and France. Even some of the precious islands of the Caribbean, prized for their suitability to produce sugar were lost to the French, the British and even the Dutch.

★

THE CENTURY OF DISCOVERY

The Spanish explorers and conquistadors launched out into an almost frantic century of discovery. In a few short decades they had traveled the length of the Andes and marched north from Mexico to the Rockies. Founding missions on the ruins of conquered native villages they actively pursued a policy of replacing all the diverse native cultures with their own. The exploits of such notables as Cabeza de Vaca, Hernando de Soto and Francisco de Coronado traveled further and saw more than any European since Marco Polo. They filled books with their stories and established Spain as one of the greatest patrons of discovery of all time.

Following the explorers and conquistadors came the true colonizers such as Pedor Menendez in Florida and Don Juan de Onate in New Mexico. These second-generation Spanish colonials spread not only the influence but also the power of Spain into areas it would occupy for hundreds of years. They built viable colonies that came to be the homes to many thousands of Spanish colonials and their Indian wards. An important part of this effort was the mission system which turned the Indians into Hispanics and the undeveloped land into productive real estate.

These efforts were not without perils. Many Spaniards lost their lives spreading the empire and capitalizing upon the fact that Spain was the first to arrive in the New World. Countless Native Americans lost their lives, their lands and their way of life to disease, war and slavery. The greatest effort made against Spain by the Native Americans to redress the wrongs done to them after the fall of the great empires was the Pueblo revolt.

Disputes between the government officials and the Mission system friars led to a loss of respect and fear on the part of the Native Americans for the Spanish. Declining populations and constant war with the tribes of the plains combined with several severe droughts led to a precipitous collapse of the food supply. This in turn led to mass starvation among the Pueblo Indians. The Spanish were at the same time attempting to destroy what they thought were the last remnants of the native religion by arresting and whipping the shaman priests.

In 1680 almost the entire population of 17,000 Pueblo Indians rose up and slaughtered every Spaniard they could finds. Their leader Pope' told them that they could recover their former health and prosperity by destroying the churches and missions of the Christians. The initial victory over the Spanish was tempered by the revival of ancient rivalries between the different Pueblo tribes. The Spanish regrouped in El Paso under Diego de Vargas and in 1691 were able to recapture New Mexico as far north as Santa Fe. Farther west the Hopi and the Zuni were able to hold out and maintain their independence providing a safety valve for the re-conquered people of the Rio Grande valley.

THE FIRST FRENCH AND INDIAN WAR

While the Spanish claimed all of North America their practical power did not extend far north of what is today the border between Florida and Georgia. In Europe the power of Spain forced the English and the French to diplomatically deny for some time that they were in fact seeking to found colonies in the Americas. The first colonies of both powers were strategically placed in the interior close to but off the coast to avoid detection and destruction. As the sixteenth century progressed, the power of Spain waned as the power of England, France and the Netherlands expanded. By 1541 the King of Spain decided not to attempt to stop the French from founding a colony along the St. Lawrence. This opened the flood gates and soon all these secondary powers began working to establish their own empires in North America.

The Spanish gave the coldness of the climate and the poverty of the land as their reasons for allowing others to build colonies in lands they claimed as their own. And the lack of ready plunder from defenseless natives and of easy-to-exploit precious metals did make the first expeditions of the new comers unprofitable since those two things were what they were seeking. However, as time went on, the French took the lead in the fur trade quickly followed by the English and the Dutch. Then the English discovered that they could make fortunes growing tobacco for export to a rapidly growing European market.

The French, English and Dutch did not conquer the Native Americans as the Spanish did; they instead began by entering into alliances and trading agreements. The many tribes of the eastern portion of North America's vast woodland were divided into two distinct groups roughly founded on language, the Algonquians and the Iroquoian. Both groups were often rivals within their respective divisions and often between each other. The alignment of these groups came to play a very important part in the shape of the growing colonies.

The fur trade quickly rose to become the greatest source of financial gain for the Europeans and the greatest source of trade goods for the Indians. And both sides soon came to depend upon the other in more ways than either could have ever imagined. As the Indians spread out further and further seeking the furs and skins the European desired they began to neglect their traditional sources of strength as they depleted their own lands and lusted for the lands of others. In addition as they became more dependent on manufactured goods, they began to lose the skills they had developed over centuries to live off the land. It even reached the point that if trade goods were cut-off, the Indians faced starvation. This became so pronounced that the Indians came to consider a cut-off of trade as a declaration of war.

Tribes who lived closest to a source of trade goods began to conquer and plunder tribes that lived further away using their monopoly on firearms to their advantage. These disruptions spread the influence and impact of the European settlements to Native Americans who never saw a colonist. The destruction of the beaver also had a dramatic impact on the environment as the previously ubiquitous lakes and ponds formed by beaver dams disappeared. These ponds and lakes had been an important source of water and habitat for other animals and as they dried up the patterns of wildlife changed forever.

In addition, the diseases of the Europeans decimated the native population in some places creating the wilderness the Europeans have always said was there. It weakened many tribes so much they merged with others and their independent history ended often after many generations of existence. And there was also alcohol. Indians had always brewed a type of beer but they had never distilled hard liquor. The impact of this import had a debilitating effect on individuals and cultures that was often purposefully exploited by the Europeans.

The French were the early leaders. They followed the St. Lawrence River more than 1,000 miles into the interior of the continent opening trade with hitherto untouched regions. They made fortunes exporting a huge volume of furs and pelts. At first it was so lucrative a trade that they did not even want to establish permanent colonies for fear of disrupting the natives and the gathering of furs. However, in 1608 Quebec was founded and soon some permanent settlers began to fan out through the vast area France claimed as their own. France soon became embroiled in the many wars of their Indian allies. They were allied with the Algonquians and Huron making enemies of the Five Nation Iroquois. The introduction of firearms into the traditional Indian warfare led to radical changes in tactics. They went from massed formations to hit and run styles. It also convinced the tribes that they needed to attain firearms above all or face defeat.

THE FIVE NATION IROQUOIS

Unfortunately for the French, they had aligned themselves with the first people they had come into contact with, which can easily be understood as a means of gaming furs fast and easy but when looked at from a strategic standpoint it made little sense. The Northern Algonquians and the Montagnais were hunter gatherers with no permanent settlements and little surplus of any kind. The Huron, an Iroquoian speaking people, were possessors of advanced horticulture and lived in large well-fortified villages. But all of them together were no match for the unified might of the Five Nation Iroquois. This confederation of tribes possessed the strongest military and the most advanced social system in North America since the demise of the ancient races of the Southwest and the Mound Builders of the Mississippi basin.

The tribes of the Northeast had long histories of warfare and the introduction of the Europeans into the mix merely changed the weapons and the tactics.

The strategy remained the same: gain land and captives which could be adopted into the tribe thereby making it bigger and its enemies smaller. The Five Nations were the best organized and the largest. They had been the most powerful and stable of all the Indian alliances in the area before the Europeans came and they remained so for centuries after.

Shortly after the first French intervention in the wars between the Huron and the Iroquois, the Dutch arrived. They soon established themselves along the Hudson River and began supplying the Five Nations with arms. This leveled the playing field and soon the French and their Indian allies were in full retreat as the Five Nations flexed their muscles to the north. The long lasting enmity between the French and the Five Nations would not be extinguished until the final fall of New France.

The Jesuits followed the French as the religious order that made the strongest inroads amongst the Indians, especially the Huron. Many Huron villages became Christian as did large numbers of the people. This made for many disagreements and disputes among the tribe. Many wanted to retain their traditional beliefs and life styles while others seeing the power of the Europeans wanted to adapt to the changing circumstances. This dissension led to aggressive actions on the part of the Five Nations. Seeing the opportunity to crush their ancient enemies and to obtain many captives, they mounted sustained attacks, eventually leading to the complete destruction of the Huron nation.

★

THE OLD DOMINION

Between the Spanish to the South and the French to the North the English sought to carve out their own colonies in what they called "Virginia" named for the virgin queen Elizabeth I. The English relied on private investors operating under royal permission to found colonies that were some of the first international joint stock companies. These promoters sought the quick riches of conquest and gold. But instead they found themselves in an area with a climate which initially proved deadly to Europeans and a land that had no easily obtainable minerals and that wouldn't grow the preferred money crop, sugar.

In addition, after a false start at Roanoke, they decided to try to establish themselves at Jamestown within the territory of a large tribal power known as the Powhatan Confederacy. The first years of the colony were ones of short lives and brutal work. Most people were either indentured servants who were worked to death or gentlemen who refused to work. The colony needed constant infusions of people to make up for the large death rate.

Emerging from a series of wars and revolutions the British Isles had eventually been unified under the scepter of the English monarch. The social structure was a carryover from feudal times; a steep pyramid with many poor on the bottom and a few wealthy at the top. Several occurrences such as the Civil War had begun to empower Parliament and mitigate the suffering of the people. The franchise was exclusively for men with property but at least the Monarchy was no longer absolute and the beginnings of a democratic structure were growing. The enclosure of the land to facilitate animal husbandry as opposed to crops left many former peasants landless and uprooted from their homes. These became the grist for the colonial mill supplying a large pool of ready workers and easy transplants.

The colonists eventually grew in number and after the introduction of tobacco, they had a cash crop. Spreading out quickly within a generation, they were hundreds of miles into the interior, building forts and plantations. The freed indentured servants built new towns and constantly pushed deeper and deeper into the continent. When the Indians had finally had enough, it was too late. The wars against the Indians cost the lives of many colonists but they decimated the Indians. By the 1670s, there were more than 40,000 colonists and they were pushing the Indians back and out through the piedmont and into the foothills of the Blue Ridge Mountains.

★

THE COLONIES BY THE BAY

While England was ruled by landed nobles and people of refined education and manners Virginia and the colonies of the Chesapeake Bay area were ruled by merchants and mechanics that worked hard and made something of themselves in a new land. It was a meritocracy instead of an aristocracy. The rise and fall of tobacco prices spelled boom and bust for these colonies that depended upon the tobacco crop for almost all their cash.

The great distance from the motherland and the growing wealth and independence of the colonists combined to establish commonwealths wherein the Royal Governor (Virginia) or Proprietor (Maryland) had to contend with the local powers to govern. These local powers became so pronounced that at one point the Assembly of Virginia arrested a confrontational governor and shipped him home. This situation led the colonists to come to expect personal freedom and rights that common Englishmen had never known.

The amount of people compared to the amount of work that needed to be done made labor a premium commodity. Compared to England where most people couldn't find a decent way to make a living, in the Chesapeake colonies, anyone willing to work could always keep busy and make a profit. And as is always the case in the presence of a free economy, the enterprising prospered building businesses for themselves.

This independence led to defiance of the crown and in more than one instance open rebellion. The most famous of all being Bacon's Rebellion, which for a time seemed destined to take over the colony of Virginia until the untimely death of Mr. Bacon after which the crown reasserted its authority. The Chesapeake colonies recovered from their spate of rebellion, built upon their freedom and their growing economy to develop a society headed by great planters and built upon yeoman farmers.

The blight upon the Chesapeake colonies was the institution of chattel slavery first imposed upon Native Americans and then upon imported Africans. This system seemed to make sense to the planters because the Africans adapted to the climate better and could work harder. But it warped the realities of the economy and the society, creating a false sense of solidarity between the planters and the yeoman in opposition to the slaves. This stopped the yeoman from seeking to democratize the system and inculcated an inherent racism that became the bane of the area for generations.

★

THE GREAT MIGRATION AND
THE BIBLE COMMONWEALTH

Originally it was considered the northern part of Virginia. Then after a few unsuccessful attempts at colonization that froze and starved their way to failure it was considered an undesirable place to attempt a colony. Then Captain John Smith of Jamestown fame made a voyage there and published a popular travelogue including a map and a new name "New England" which enticed colonists into believing it was a fair approximation of Old England across the pond and it became an enduring success.

The English Puritans were followers of the Protestant reformation. They believed that the Church of England which had been founded by King Henry VIII when he was unable to obtain a divorce from the Pope retained too much of the rights and rituals of the Catholic Church. They might be called purists. They wanted simple services and plain churches. The Church of England retained statues, stained glass windows, golden crosses, ministers they called "Priests" and "Father" adorned in splendid vestments.

In the sixteenth and seventeenth centuries the Church of England was the "Established" church. Meaning it was a part of the state. The King or Queen was (and is) the head of the church no matter how worldly they were or even if they didn't believe in God. They appointed the Archbishop of Canterbury and all the other Bishops. Every citizen was required to support and attend the church. The clergy were paid by the state. The church courts were often used by the state to punish people that the government suspected of disloyalty to the crown. As in all countries with established churches the ideas of heresy and treason became confounded.

Many puritans wanted to remain active members of the established church and reform it from within. Other wanted to immediately separate and form their own pure congregations; these were known as separatists and they were the object of sporadic and often horrendous persecution. Some of the separatists left the country, many finding sanctuary in Holland where the religious toleration allowed them to worship as they wished.

Socially the Puritans believed in what they saw as the Biblical principles of thrift, diligence and hard work. They were mostly from the middleclass and had much more than the majority of Englishmen who were struggling just to get by. When persecution rose to a crescendo in the 1620s and 1630s the Puritans were finally spurred to action. The Massachusetts Bay Company was founded in London by people who had remained in the Church of England and were able to operate within the legal structure of the day. They sought and received a royal charter to found a colony in the New World. This is where they did something entirely different than the Virginia Company which maintained itself in England as a limited liability company which had shareholders and used its resources to send out expeditions and settlers hoping for a profit. Instead of operating after the model previously established by the Virginia Company, the Massachusetts Bay Company relocated to the New World thus establishing itself as self-governing colony with only nominal connection to the royal government.

Landing in an area where a great plague of European diseases had swept away the Native population, the Puritans were able to move into deserted villages and plant in abandoned fields. They saw it as the providence of God. The Natives obviously saw it as something altogether different. The Puritan colonists were by nature hardworking and frugal and so had a much easier time establishing a self-sufficient colony than did the indolent and wealth-seeking colonists in Virginia. In addition, there was a huge influx of people, men, women and children, whole families that not only added to the population but were also able to multiply it quickly. Within a few decades, by 1640, they were already spreading out and founding secondary colonies such as Connecticut, Rhode Island and New Hampshire.

Land was granted to groups of people who banded together to find towns. These lands were then held in common and divided among the families according to the wishes of the town. The colony would outline the town's area but they left it up to the towns to decide upon their internal policies. The land needed clearing and tending. The livestock needed pasture and each village divided the land and managed as they saw fit. Women were accorded equal status in religious matters except the posts of leadership, teaching and preaching, which means they were able to be saved, join the church and work but only men could lead. However, women in New England had more rights and privileges than women in the Chesapeake Colonies.

When the Great Migration ended in the 1640s an economic depression followed the cessation of this constant infusion of new people and money. And this is when the commerce which was to make New England famous around the world began to manifest itself. First the fishing banks of the coast were exploited for local consumption as well as for export to Europe. Next, the great and developing agricultural surplus was soon being shipped to Europe as well. Building upon the abundant resources, shipbuilding was soon an expanding industry, building both ships for the coastal trade and ocean-going vessels.

THE BIBLE COMMONWEALTH

The Puritans saw their earthly mission to build God's kingdom on earth. The Puritans followed the beliefs of the other reformers that everyone should read and know the Bible for themselves. Therefore, printing was an early and an important industry for there was a constant call for more Bibles and other study materials. There were many more churches and more preachers in New England than in Virginia. Since church attendance and hearing the educated preachers was a major source of the education of the day, when combined with the higher level of literacy required to read the Bible for themselves, the level of education was consequently much higher in New England than in the Chesapeake Colonies.

The insular aspects of the Puritan colonies led to disputes with the non-Puritans who were inevitably drawn to a successful colony. The purity of the colony was diluted by those who came after. The laws had to be loosened to fit the changing circumstances and there were also those who just had different ideas. There were Baptists and Quakers, Anglicans and Catholics, all of which were attracted by the material success but who wanted a more inclusive vision. Nontraditional leaders such as Anne Hutchinson, one of the founders of Rhode Island and occurrences such as the witchcraft trails combined to split the once unified and relatively homogeneous New England into competing visions for a fractious future.

It may have faltered as a shining city on a hill and it certainly didn't create heaven on earth, but it was a successful model for a flourishing colony. Materially prosperous and politically independent, New England held out a promise that the New World could become something that really was new.

THE INDIAN POLICY OF NEW ENGLAND

The Puritans didn't see the land they colonized as pristine, which it wasn't, and they didn't see it as merely undeveloped, which it wasn't; instead they saw it as a "hideous and desolate wilderness full of wild beasts and wild men." With such an outlook is it any wonder that they looked upon the land as something to be conquered? Is it any wonder that they looked upon the Native Americans as inferior members of an inferior culture to be shunted aside at best and eliminated at worst?

The Native Americans the Puritans encountered in New England were mainly from the Algonquian linguistic group. They were divided along linguistic lines by dialect and along clan lines by families. The main groups subdivided over and over and there was much individual freedom to move between groups along these inter-relational lines. They possessed the same advanced horticultural techniques which were almost universal along the Eastern coast of North America. They grew the same crops and used the same weapons as the Natives encountered by the English in Virginia but they did not have the same level of political development. There were no great confederations like the Five Nations or the Powhatan. And so the Puritans did not have to fit into local power structures as the least powerful and newest entrants on a varied and dynamic political stage. Instead they moved into abandoned villages left empty by the ravages of European imported diseases and claimed well cleared fields left fallow by the death of their owners. They even went so far as to say God had cleared out the heathen so they could enter in, and they believed it was true.

At a very early point the growing Puritan colonies began pushing the Indians out of more and more land. They saw every agreement on the part of the natives as an abject acceptance of English sovereignty. They used trade goods and the ability to traverse great distances between various tribes as a means to not only capture much of the intertribal trade but also to use it to their advantage playing one tribe against another.

A prime example of the exploitation of rivalry is found in the history of the Pequot War. The usual story is that the Pequot were recent invaders who came in and mercilessly subjugated the local Mohegan and Narragansett and that the New English merely aided them in freeing themselves from the hated oppressors. In reality the Puritans wanted to incorporate the lands of the Pequot into their growing commonwealth and to do so they lured the other Indians into guiding them to the isolated Pequot villages.

The traditional mode of combat among the Indians was long on show and short on mayhem. They sought to capture women and children to incorporate them into their tribes to make themselves stronger and their enemies weaker. They did not engage in wholesale slaughter and the general conquest of the lands of others but that is just what they signed on for in the Pequot War. In less than two years' time the Puritans had so decimated the tribe that they declared the Pequot to have ceased to exist as a tribe. Later they resurrected the Pequot by convincing some who had been adopted into the Narragansett to once again reconstitute their tribe as allies of the Puritans in a war against the Narragansett. One side against the other until the Puritans were the only side left.

MISSIONARY ACTIVITIES
AND PRAYING TOWNS

Pushed and prodded by their fellow believers back in England the Puritans began actively attempting to evangelize the Indians beginning in the late 1640s. Many members of the smaller and weaker bands of Indians had decided that it was foolish to try and resist the ever-increasing English and so they sought protection and advancement by adopting Christianity and following European ways. They gathered together in large inter-tribal villages known as "Praying Towns" where they could learn from the English and begin to gain the advancements that civilization had to offer. Though the larger and most powerful of the tribes never found the Praying Towns or the missionaries appealing these towns did grow and become an important part of the Puritan scene in Massachusetts. This venture eventually crashed against the shoals of the bloodiest war ever fought between the Indians and the Puritans.

KING PHILLIP'S WAR

Victors write History. This is a reality which has colored the perception of events since the First Emperor of China made himself the first emperor by destroying all the records of anything that had gone before. Thus it is with "King Phillip's War." King Phillip wasn't even the name of the man the Puritan's have immortalized as the Machiavellian leader of the coordinated attack against the innocent English in 1675.

After seizing the land and displacing the cultures of the many tribes and bands who were the original possessors of the land the Puritans began acting in a very high-handed manner by imposing their laws and conventions on the members of any and all tribes in their vicinity. In the spring of 1675, they arrested and hanged several Indians who had killed an Indian from one of the Praying Towns who was considered a traitor by other Indians for guiding the English to their camps.

This act of self-declared sovereignty over the people of another nation led to spontaneous reactions from the Indians. These people believed in blood feuds and retribution, revenge raids and reciprocity and the Indians who were hung all had relatives and friends. Soon many of the tribes joined in a massive effort to rid their lands of the ever more intrusive English, but it was too late.

The Great Migration and a prodigious birth rate had increased the English population to the point that they easily outnumbered all the local tribes together.

The technological advantage had been lost. Greedy traders had ignored the law against selling firearms to Indians and they had gained flintlock rifles and become very adept at using them. However, the English, held a monopoly on the repair of broken firearms and the production of gunpowder. In addition, contrary to the myth which has been perpetrated and preserved, the English held an overwhelming advantage in organization. The tribes never united. Each tribe fought under their own leaders in their own way for their own goals. The English on the other hand immediately ceased their petty disputes and stood united against the tribes.

The Indians sought to cleanse their land by destroying every visage of the Europeans. They burned buildings, knocked down fences and killed livestock. They were so intent on cleansing the land that they even killed many families including women and children contrary to their own custom of adopting women and children. They had learned the lesson of total war from the English during the Pequot War and they were using that knowledge to restore their sovereignty in the land that had once been their own.

The Indians had also adapted their tactics as well as their strategy. Instead of fighting in massed formations with great displays to prove their bravery they set ambushes and fought a guerrilla-style campaign that proved highly effective since they knew the terrain so much better than their enemies. They would stage a surprise attack and then retreat. When they were pursued they would set ambushes choosing the place to fight and inflicting heavy casualties on their pursuers. In frustration at not being able to find or defeat their foes the English turned against the Indians of the Praying Towns attacking and killing the defenseless Christianized Indians because they could.

Eventually, the English learned a valuable lesson. They abandoned their traditional European-style tactics of massed formations and adopted the same guerilla-style as the Indians which worked so well in the thick forests and swamps. Using other Indians as guides and scouts they were soon inflicting serious losses on the tribes and whereas the English could absorb the losses they had sustained and rebound the Indians could not. When the food supplies or equipment of the Indians was destroyed in a raid, they could not requisition replacements from the coast as the English could. Instead they starved. When they ran out of shot and powder they couldn't get more from their storehouses; they had to retreat before the firepower of the English.

The Mohawk Indians, one of the Five Nation Iroquois, also allied themselves with the English seeing this as a perfect opportunity to smash their longtime rivals, the Algonquians. As the tribes began to surrender one by one, the war fizzled to a close when Metacom, the man immortalized as King Phillip, was killed by one of the Praying Town Indians in the service of the English. The Puritans cut off Metacom's head and mounted it on a pike at Plymouth as a warning to all who would dare resist their conquest of New England, and thus died the hopes, dreams and memories of the proud Indian nations who had once owned the land.

★

THE CROWN JEWEL

The seventeenth century saw the rise of the West Indies to become the most important colonies of England. They were the most important because they produced abundant crops of sugar and sugar was what greased the financial wheels for the entire colonial enterprise. It afforded the profits and covered the losses to fuel a growing empire and the navy needed to make it happen.

The islands of the West Indies had been ignored by the Spanish as too small to bother with and they were consequently claimed and settled first by pirates from the three later colonizing powers, England, France and Holland and then colonized by settlers eager to prosper in the New World. With Barbados as their hub, the English soon filled these islands with plantations. In a short time, there were more colonists in the West Indies than in the Chesapeake and

New England colonies combined which made sense since the financial rewards were also greater.

The same pattern was followed as in the Chesapeake Colonies. At first the majority of colonists came as indentured servants who once they were free sought to build their own holdings into sugar-producing plantations. Then when it proved economically profitable the planters began importing African slaves. The Africans proved to be much better suited to the climate and able to survive much better than the indentured servants plus they never had to be freed. The West Indies were the first English colonies to have a majority slave population. This demographic fact is evident in the current population of the Islands. The slave codes or laws as with the work and climate were particularly harsh, all of which lead to high mortality rates among the slaves and a consequently high rate of importation of more Africans to swell the constantly thinning workforce.

In contrast to the wretched existence of the majority of the population which were slaves the apex of society was held by the great planters. Growing sugar was an expensive proposition if it was going to pay. In other words, it takes money to make money. As time went on, the land in the West Indies became more and more concentrated in the hands of a small minority of great planters who bought or muscled out the smaller ones. These Great Planters became fabulously wealthy and lived in a grand style in opulent homes surrounded by the finest imports from Europe.

Besides sugar which was refined and processed into raw sugar, molasses and rum, the West Indies also produced a highly sought-after grade of tobacco. All in all, the West Indies were without a doubt the jewel in the crown of English colonialism.

★

ONE BECOMES TWO

Unlike the other English colonies in North America, the Carolinas were established under the auspices of the Lords Proprietors by West Indian planters. The Lords Proprietors, eight extremely rich men were based in London and they wanted experienced colonists to ensure the success of their financial venture.

Many of the rich planters of the West Indies did not want to divide their land between multiple heirs. They instead followed a strict enforcement of primogeniture leaving everything to the eldest son. Daughters were of course married off but younger sons found it hard to make their way and the Carolinas offered a great opportunity to set them up in great style and add to the family wealth at the same time.

However there was a potential problem. Founding a society of great planters on a frontier had its dangers.

The planters were afraid that their slaves would run off into the wilds and perhaps join with the Indians to fight against them. To avoid this they devised an ingenious plan to at the least keep the slaves and the Indians apart. And at best make them mortal enemies. To accomplish their purpose, they made treaties with the Indians providing them with weapons and other trade goods for returning run-away slaves.

THE COLONISTS

Though this was a society designed to be a steep pyramid led by a small group of very rich planters who started at the top and had every intention of staying there, the colonists were on the whole a diverse lot. There were rich, poor and in-between. There were Great Planters, tradesmen and indentured servants. They came from the West Indies and from England. What they had in common was the opportunity to shape a fertile land that seemed vast and open to people accustomed to the confined space of the West Indian islands and the crowded cities of England. The Lords Proprietors were generous in their grants of land from the great estates given to the Planters to the relatively large plots given to the indentured servants who survived their years of labor. Some of these former servants were able to rise to the top ranks of society and this mobility was something that could not be equaled in either England or the West Indies.

The independence and prosperous settlements around the Albemarle Sound, which had been founded by Virginians didn't like the idea that they were included in the royal grant to the Lord Proprietors and thus a part of Carolina ruled from Charles Town. This discontent finally led to the split between North and South Carolina in 1712.

From its founding, the Lord Proprietors ruled Carolina as a personal possession. Yes, they were generous in their grants of land; however, since this land really belonged to the Indians and had been granted to the Lord Proprietors by a King who had never seen them, they proved the rule that it is easy to be generous with the belongings of others. This generosity did not however extend to actual control of the colony.

THE COUP

In 1719 the Assembly of South Carolina exhibited the independence which would mark its character ever since. Feeling that the Lords Proprietors far off in London were hopelessly unconnected to the affairs of the colony, the Assembly revolted and declared themselves to be the governing authority of the colony authorized by the people to take control of governmental affairs. Recognizing the reality of the situation in 1729, the crown purchased all the rights of the Lords Proprietors and converted the Carolinas into royal colonies. The crown only exercised minimal control, appointing governors and regulating international trade. This exchange of the Colonial Assembly for the Lords Proprietors consolidated the power of the Great Planters. It was they who usually filled the Assembly and it was their children and clients who also filled the courts and the bureaucracies. Often it seemed as if the major object of the colonial government was adjudicating the growth of plantations and the maintenance of the Carolina's ridged slave laws.

CAROLINA'S UNIQUE INDIAN POLICY

While in most colonies it was one of the principle points of policy to prevent weapons, especially firearms and ammunition from falling into the hands of Indians, the leaders in Carolina came up with a novel approach. As mentioned earlier, one major concern for the planters was the fear that their large slave population would combine with the indigenous people and overwhelm the greatly outnumbered Caucasians. To forestall this, they came up with the policy that would live in infamy as the Gun Trade.

Here's how it worked. Instead of working rigorously to keep firearms out of the hands of the Indians the colonists chose powerful local tribes and armed them. Initially this was to use for enlarging the natives' ability to obtain furs and skins for trade. Then as time and relationships progressed the colonists engaged the Indians to catch runaway slaves paying for the slaves with more guns. Exploiting the Indians tradition of taking members of other tribes as captives the colonists were also willing to purchase Indian captives which they would send to the West Indies to sell as slaves, thereby making money while at the same time reducing the number of Indians they had to contend with.

This policy caused the tribe being armed to vault to the top of the local power pyramid. Immediately, they would begin expanding their territory and raiding as far afield as they could to obtain furs, skins, runaway slaves and captives. These sparked innumerable wars among the tribes further destabilizing them and making them less able to stand up to the constantly expanding colony.

Eventually the first tribes armed started to need more

weapons, powder and shot than they could pay for, so they went into debt. When the debt became substantial enough the colonists would arm another tribe and become their allies against the first tribe while at the same time cutting off weapons, repairs and supplies to the first tribe. Soon tribe number two was bringing tribe number one as captives and now they were on the boat to the West Indies. In time, the process was repeated with tribe number three against number two and four against three until the Indian problem was solved.

This ingenious way of subverting an entire race spread the influence of the Carolina colony through the Piedmont and into the Blue Ridge Mountains, through the southern plain all the way to the Mississippi as tribes using their technical advantage to attack tribes further out seizing furs, skins, hunting lands and captives. The slaves were intimidated by the ferocious army of armed men waiting for the opportunity to catch and return them if they managed to escape.

The French used an intimate cultural knowledge and the willingness to share the life style of the Native Americans to gain allies and friends. The Spanish sought to turn the Native Americans into Hispanics, seeking to convert them into taxpaying subjects. The English of the Chesapeake colonies or New England sought to overwhelm and conquer the natives, clearing the land through attrition. Only the colonists of Carolina hit upon the idea of using their economic advantage to pay the Native Americans to destroy themselves.

ECONOMICS

Mercantilism was the theory that was dominant in Europe during the seventeenth and eighteenth centuries. It held that the wealth of a nation depended on its possession of precious metals. In practice this meant that the governments of Europe sought to maximize foreign trade surpluses by promoting national commercial interests, building a powerful navy and a large merchant marine. These were then used to establish colonies which were seen as sources of raw materials and markets for manufactured products.

As with any colony in an empire based upon the economic theory of mercantilism, Carolina had to find a way to not only provide a place for people to live but also a way to produce exports to add to the wealth of the homeland. Adapting quickly to the land and its resources, the people of the Carolinas initially became a primary source for the lumber and tar so necessary to ship building and of vital importance to an empire built and sustained by a large and growing navy and merchant marine.

Next, they excelled in the production of cattle and pigs using the warm marshes and nut-rich forests to free range their livestock even though it caused irreparable harm to the open fields of the Indians' extensive horticulture-based society. However, though these early successes proved the worth of the colony and provided much-needed capital for expansion, they still needed a cash crop. Virginia had tobacco. New England had fish. The Carolina found theirs when they tried growing rice in the humid and rich low lands of the coastal region. Soon the planters were draining swamps and moving forward to become the rice bowl of the English Empire.

This lucrative enterprise soon afforded the Great Planters a lavish lifestyle rivaling their forefathers in the West Indies and surpassing even what many English Lords were able to sustain. Their homes, their clothes, furniture and jewels were becoming the stuff of legend. Conversely the great rice plantations were built on the homelands of Indian tribes, seizing their towns, hunting lands and sacred places. The growth of the rice plantations also caused untold suffering for the tens of thousands of slaves who toiled and died in the disease-infested swamps that had been turned into rice paddies. Caucasians were soon the minority in the colony as the slave population swelled. The Great Planters through the Assembly, they controlled enacted increasingly stringent slave codes to keep their victims enthralled. While the planters boasted of the liberty they had obtained through their successful coup and their resulting rule by Assembly they kept the majority of the population in abject poverty, ignorance and terror.

GEORGIA

No story of the Carolinas can be complete without also sharing the founding of Georgia.

To secure England's hold on the increasingly prosperous Carolinas, it was decided to found a colony between the thriving new colony and the Spanish holdings in Florida. Spain was still a formidable power and she still claimed the land to the north of her Florida holdings.

In the past Spanish raiding parties had ranged up and down the Atlantic coast looking for the interlopers.

The effort to found a buffer colony was led by several wealthy philanthropists headed by James Oglethorpe and collectively known as the Georgia Trustees. It was their intent to accomplish what the Virginia Company had originally said was one of their main goals; provide a place for the rehabilitation and succor of England's urban poor. Receiving a charter for twenty-one years, the Trustees had almost total control until the colony would automatically revert to the crown and become a royal colony. The Trustees invested their own money, raised charitable donations and also received grants from the crown and the parliament to finance their experiment. James Oglethorpe led the first colonists personally: however, he had no plans to remain in America and after establishing the first few outposts, returned to London.

Seeking to maximize the number of small yeoman farmers and minimize the number of large plantations, the Trustees at first limited people to fifty-acre tracts. They also hoped this would limit the numbers of slaves since it would not be economically viable to maintain slaves with only fifty acres. They also made the importation or owning of slaves illegal. Another of their innovations was to restrict the growth of rice which required a plantation system and instead encourage the growth of hemp for rope, mulberries for silk worms and silk production, grapes and other crops that didn't require vast holdings but did require diligent farmers. The goal was to inspire tightly knit densely populated settlements which would provide the large militias needed to protect a long and exposed frontier surrounded by antagonistic tribes and a hostile Spain.

CONCLUSION

As the only English colony to outlaw slavery, Georgia was at the forefront of liberation and freedom in America but the experiment was not to last. Soon planters from Carolina were migrating and establishing outposts in the territory. Soon, the English colonists wanted to emulate the genteel society and thriving economy of Carolina. The Trustees tried to keep the lid on things by restricting the consumption of rum, and the avocation of lawyers among other things. However the great distance and the lack of understanding of the colonial experience on the part of the Trustees opened a wedge between them and their wards that grew greater and greater as time went on.

Eventually the divide escalated into open rebellion as the colonists sought liberty and property rights, including the right to own larger holdings and slaves. Even before the twenty-one years expired, the Trustees capitulated to the rising demands and surrendered their rights, and so Georgia reverted to the crown, becoming a virtual clone of the Carolinas.

★

THE PLACE IN-BETWEEN

Between the Chesapeake Colonies and New England there existed an expanse of coast and its associated hinterlands that would soon join the English holdings and become known collectively as the Middle Colonies. They had a better climate than New England and were healthier than the Chesapeake region. They proved extremely well suited for growing grains and raising cattle. They soon boasted a large and growing population.

Initially however this population wasn't made up of the English. They ignored the area for the first part of the seventeenth century finding the New England venture and the Chesapeake area enough to keep them busy. In the interim the Dutch established a flourishing New Netherland along the Hudson River and the Swedes built their New Sweden along the Delaware. The English weren't happy about this incursion in an area they considered their own but they did not directly confront either rival immediately for two reasons. One, they were not strong enough, and two, both of their new world rivals were their Old World friends. Both Sweden and the Netherlands were Protestant powers and both were valuable allies in the religious wars and power diplomacy of the times.

In the latter half of the seventeenth century, things changed. For one thing, the Dutch had swallowed New Sweden and then the Dutch, who were now England's main commercial rival in Europe and world-wide, were swallowed in turn by the expanding English, New Netherlands being renamed; New York in 1664.

Unlike the Spanish, French and Dutch the English crown exerted little direct power over their colonies. Following the tenants of mercantilism to their logical conclusions, they instead sought commercial benefit through taxation and the belief that every raw material such as wood or tar that they could produces at home or in a colony made them stronger. Also, they did not fund the colonies out of the royal treasury as the other European colonizing powers did. Instead the cash-strapped English relied upon private enterprise and entrepreneurship leading to what many think is the greatest contribution of the British Empire to economics, the limited liability corporation. This left much latitude and personal individuality to the separate colonies and also had a great influence on the future development of the United States.

Besides the commercial tradition of free enterprise, this situation also had a profound impact on the political developments in the English colonies. All except New

England were controlled by absentee proprietors who were thousands of miles away and often extremely short of cash. The colonists as they became firmly established and self-sufficient, following in a long line of English tradition, began to flex their economic muscle and the power of the purse to increase their political leverage. They wrested concession from the proprietors in the form of autonomous assemblies with real power to shape local events. They also sought control of courts and customs. In some cases they even staged coups such as in Carolina declaring pseudo-independence or as in Georgia where they appealed to the crown for protection from the leadership guidelines or strictures of the absentee proprietors.

A special case was New England. As stated earlier, the proprietors were wealthy Puritans who formed the Massachusetts Bay Company which actually relocated to the colonies. Having a royal charter themselves and having the principles of the company as actual participating members of the colony made them in everything but name independent and they acted as if they were in fact independent, asking no leave and taking every privilege. They developed republican forms such as their famous town meetings and looked to no one besides themselves and God for all they wanted, needed or desired.

Gradually as the proprietors found themselves in financial problems they turned to the crown for a bail-out. The price of this help always came with strings and eventually the crown gained not only control but also title of colony after colony. The Puritans even began to fear that the royal fist was next going to aim at them. But instead the crown was diverted by the rich prize which lay just to the south of the semi-independent New England. In 1664 a mighty fleet of English warships descended upon the future port and near perfect harbor of New Amsterdam ascending the Hudson and conquering New Netherland.

The Dutch had built an American empire that was thriving by the time it was appropriated by the English. It was anchored by the growing community of New Amsterdam located at the mouth of the Hudson River. This city was founded initially to provide a secure transport hub for the furs coming down river from Fort Orange and the extensive and valuable trade with the Five Nations of the Iroquois Confederation. As time moved, the Dutch expanded their presence, building farms along the river to supply their colonists with food. These farms soon had a surplus that became a valuable export being used mainly to feed other Dutch colonists in the West Indies. The Dutch colony was prosperous and growing when it was suddenly plucked like a ripe fruit by the English. It was however a small colony on the fringe of a vast worldwide empire and the overextended Dutch had to pick their battles carefully so they did not attempt to retake the colony.

A small nation of only 1.5 million the Dutch had risen in a relatively short time from being a province of Spain to the greatest commercial empire in the world boasting the greatest navy. While the religious wars wracked Europe and while the other European powers were all united to counterbalance the overwhelming preponderance of Spain, little Netherlands was safe behind its dykes and secure in the enjoyment of their wealth. However, as the religious wars subsided and as they themselves impoverished the Spaniards by stealing their treasure and conquering their outposts, others began to look at the growing power of this tiny nation as a slight against them. Soon England on the high seas and France on land began to seek ways to challenge the Dutch. In the Americas, this translated into the English conquest of New Netherlands.

This conquest had an ulterior motive. As a matter of fact, when the English fleet sailed there was speculation that it was headed for Boston to assert royal control over the semi-independent New England. Although the blow fell on the Dutch instead of the Puritans, the lesson was not lost. The crown intended to take a more active role and the establishment of a royal colony on their southern border let the Puritans know that from then on the representatives of the king would not be far away.

THE COVENANT CHAIN

Once the English supplanted the Dutch as the dominant European power and the traders at Fort Orange (renamed Albany), they took the place of the Dutch in their alliance with the Five Nation Iroquois Confederation. The two allies stood together against the French and swore to help each other against all other enemies. The Five Nations claimed to have conquered the western regions as far south as the Ohio and as far west as the furthest reaches of the Great Lakes. These claims were more hyperbole than reality but the English acknowledged them as true and by extension claimed that since they asserted their suzerainty over the Five Nation by extension they said they held title to all these far-flung territories. This was a claim the French bitterly refused to acknowledge basing their competing claims on their far-ranging exploration and the many relationships they had established with the tribes who actually controlled the territories.

The English not only traded with the Five Nations and used their boasts to expand their claims, but they also used them as enforcers with regard to the other smaller Indian nations in the area. This alliance came to be the lynch pin of English American diplomacy with regard to the relations with the Native Americans north of the Chesapeake Colonies. It was the source and the summit of power. The guns given to the Iroquois became the tip of the English lance towards any tribe that dared try to stand against them.

NEW JERSEY

The House of Stuart had ambitions of becoming absolute monarchs on the model of the French. But they were held back by English tradition and a lack of money. They did not have the vast estates and the power to tax by decree that the French monarch had. Instead they had to wheel and deal with an often intractable and always jealous parliament. One place they looked to increase their riches which would increase their power was the colonies. They wanted more royal control so they could tax the continually growing commerce. After the royal conquest of New York, it appeared that they were finally on their way to establishing direct royal control but then they took a divergent course which added to the diversity of the American colonies instead of to the size of the royal treasury.

Unable to keep a strategy headed in the right direction and almost immediately after seizing New York the King's brother the Duke of York granted a charter to two wealthy patrons for political consideration. This grant was for all the lands between the Hudson and the Delaware rivers as a separate colony called New Jersey. The reduction of royal control was further diluted when these two absentee proprietors sold off their right to two separate groups. One was headed by a Scotsman and the other group was headed by Quakers. These two groups promptly divided the colony into East and West New Jersey. The Scotts took east Jersey and the Quakers took West Jersey.

This situation lasted until 1702 when the crown reunited the two Jerseys into the royal colony of New Jersey. The fact that the proprietors retained legal title to the land led to many disputes in East Jersey due to the exorbitant rents and demands made upon the rent holders. This led to riots and to a depressed rate of economic growth which contributed to the fact that New Jersey lagged behind its neighbors both to the North and the South for generations in development and wealth.

PENNSYLVANIA

William Penn was a rich gentleman descended from a famous and well-connected admiral. He was also a creditor of the king. The always cashed-strapped Stuart King James I settled a debt with Penn by granting him 45,000 square miles of land beyond the Delaware River. This was augmented by grants from the Duke of York. Penn, a rich and grand-living Quaker, founded a colony where religious tolerance and economic opportunity soon established a thriving colony filled with industrious people. The Quakers had withstood persecution in England because they refused to take part in or support the established church. Penn himself was jailed on several occasions as an unlicensed preacher. Therefore there was a ready impetus for them to immigrate to Pennsylvania. Like the Puritans of New England, many of the settlers in Pennsylvania were families with their own resources. They were tradesmen and merchants, farmers and artisans. This type of population adapted well, worked hard and soon established growing communities ever deeper into the woods, always moving west.

William Penn was a shrewd and good administrator of his colony. He treated the Indians with respect and acknowledged them as the rightful owners of the land. He did not trick them or appropriate their land; he purchased it and he didn't allow anyone to settle on any land unless he first purchased it from the Indians. This led to a more peaceful occupation of the land than in any other colony.

The harmony of the colony was disrupted by sectional rivalries which plague the commonwealth to this day. The counties to the east are pitted against the counties to the west each always striving for their own advantage. In colonial times this could deal with the perceived need for fortifications or roads, Indian relations or economic developments. The profitable colony could not keep pace with the lavish lifestyle of its proprietor and in 1707 William Penn found himself sentenced to an English debtor prison even though he personally owned a colony bigger than some European countries.

★

Oliver Cromwell.

THE GLORIOUS BIRTH
OF GREAT BRITAIN

The always-grasping never-satisfied Stuart dynasty had a rough time during their four reigns as the kings of England. They sought for absolute power and ended up losing the constitutional power they had. The second one was beheaded by his own people and the last one was chased out of the country. The first and the third were wastrels who partied themselves to distraction and spent themselves into poverty. They are best remembered for the line applied to their restoration after the regicide and the Commonwealth of Oliver Cromwell: "They never learned anything and never forgot anything." All in all they were a sad interlude in a proud heritage.

When the people of England could suffer these inept political neophytes no longer, they rose up in what is known as the Glorious Revolution, chased James II from the country and welcomed William of Orange the husband of James' daughter Mary as the Protestant replacements to the hated Catholic James.

The coup was greeted in the colonies with jubilation on the part of those seeking greater independence. They quickly seized upon the revolution as an opportunity to cast the appointees of James as recalcitrant adherents to the old regime and themselves as ardent supporters of the new. This led to the overturning of every royal colonial government and the installation of more independent and more liberty-minded groups.

William of Orange, now styled William III of England, was a battle-hardened veteran of the long and bitter continental wars against the aggrandizements of Louis XIV. His main reason for coveting the crown of England was to subtract England from its alliance with France and to add it to his coalition against that same power. He had little concern for the colonies except as they figured into his consolidation of power in England and his mobilization of its power against France.

In consequence to this he picked and chose winners and losers in the colonial power struggles based upon his own calculations not the calculations or interests of the colonists. Sometime this coincided with colonial interests. In Pennsylvania, William suspended the charter because Penn had been a favorite of James and he thus made Pennsylvania a royal colony. In Maryland, he allowed Lord Baltimore to retain his ownership but took the government of the colonies out of his Catholic hands and put it into the hands of an appointed Protestant governor. In Massachusetts, William refused to allow a return to their original charter and he retained them as royal colonies but he allowed them a great degree of autonomy and independence in local matters. The smaller New England colonies were allowed to reinstitute their original charters.

William plunged England into a long-lasting series of European wars all designed to hobble France for the benefit of his native Holland. These wars cost England more than anyone could have imagined. They led to a level of taxation never before known to support a massive increase in the military establishment both on land and on the sea. This also meant that William and the crown were occupied elsewhere. They had precious little resources to send to America and sought nothing more than revenue to fight on in Europe. The king didn't really care what was going on in the colonies as long as they didn't cause him to divert men or material from his main theater of action and as long as they contributed money to the war effort. Under these circumstances the colonists were able to gain a degree of freedom and independence not known back in England.

During these years the crowns of England and Scotland were formally united. They had become united when James VI of Scotland was crowned as James I of England. Though united in the person of the king and still united after the regicide in the Commonwealth, they were officially united in 1707 and after that date the Scots soon came to outnumber the English as immigrants to the colonies. This marks the birth of Great Britain and the end of Scotland as an independent nation.

Another feature of the eighteenth century British Empire was it suppression of the pirates which had once been an unofficial arm of its own foreign policy against the Spanish. As the Spanish Empire declined and the British became the dominant sea power, the pirates had become more and more of a nuisance. Eventually the British used the same tactics which had always worked against pirates, sink their ships, burn their bases and hang those captured. This effectively suppressed the pirates and brought a measure of peace to the sea lanes, so a commercial empire like Britain could thrive. The British were preeminently an empire of shopkeepers and merchants. They may not have had raw political power but they held economic power that could sway the powers that be. The colonies had been founded as economic enterprises and even after most of them devolved or evolved into royal colonies, they remained primarily economic enterprises. Following the tenants of mercantilism ever uppermost in the mind of the royal government was how can the colonies benefit the homeland? How can they contribute to the power of the crown? And while the empire of the English now spread around the world, it was profoundly an Atlantic worldview that predominated the thinking of the empire builders just as it was a European worldview that had predominated the mind of King William allowing the colonies to further develop as independent-minded enclaves in the midst of a far-flung empire.

★

Le *Souverain des mers.*

THE FIRST INFORMATION HIGHWAY

That the Atlantic Ocean was a barrier between the Old World and the New World was attested to by the thousands of years the Americas lay in splendid isolation. Sporadic contact by the Norse, Irish fisherman and the stray mariner blown off course did nothing to end the nearly insurmountable barrier. Then, as the technological expertise of the Europeans advanced, as their navigation skills developed, a crack was made in the wall by Columbus. He was soon followed by larger and larger Spanish expeditions in the middle latitudes and Portuguese in the south. Soon their empires rivaled Rome and shifted the balance of power in Europe in favor of the Iberians.

The emerging powers of England, France and the Netherlands soon began to prey upon the rich Spanish, then to explore and settle on their own further north.

The initial trickle of explorers, adventurers and traders soon became a flood and then a torrent as the wealth and opportunity of the Americas beckoned.

The English built their colonies along the Eastern seaboard of North America wedged between the Spanish in Florida and the French in Canada. One after another the colonies sprang to life, Virginia, New England, the Carolinas, and the Middle Colonies all became consumers of English manufacturers and shippers of raw materials and produce. The Atlantic trade grew from a one-way supply line for precarious adventures on the edge of a wilderness into a well-oiled machine moving cargo in both directions and fueling a booming English economy. It also provided the impetus and the means to build the largest merchant fleet and the most powerful navy in the world. In less than 150 years, the Atlantic Ocean went from being a barrier to being a conduit, from being an impediment to being a facilitator, and England grew from a poor kingdom on the edge of Europe into a world-shaking empire.

DIVERSITY

An interesting demographic shift took place in the English colonies that was not paralleled in the colonies of its rivals. This was a development that would have dramatic impact on the later development of the British colonies as well as upon the subsequent growth of the United States. The growth of the colonies began to have a beneficial effect on the Homeland. The rise in exports and in the shipping trade led to a boom in the British economy which in turn led to a drop in the number of people who wanted to immigrate to the colonies. This conundrum could have led to a self-defeating spiral, however, the British came up with a novel idea; they sought to entice people of other nationalities to immigrate to their colonies.

The other European colonial powers, France, Spain and the Netherlands followed a policy of exclusion and consequently the populations of their colonies remained small and in the New World small eventually meant vulnerable. Eventually this became an instance where size really does matter because the British colonies with their much larger populations were able to absorb both the Dutch and the French colonies in North America in many ways because of their denser population.

In a Europe divided by nationality, language and custom how did the British crown manage to entice multiple tens of thousands of non-English to settle in their lands and become productive and supportive citizens? First they turned to their newly absorbed neighbor Scotland. The two countries had been united ever since James VI of Scotland became James I of England. However they had remained separate kingdoms with one king each with their own parliament, military, treasury, etc. In 1707, the two nations permanently united to form Great Britain. Enticing the Scots with a similar but better climate and more economic opportunity, they soon replaced the English as the number one source of colonists for North America.

But this was not enough to keep the boom going, so the British turned to the people of Germany. Germany at the time was divided up into many small independent kingdoms, principalities and other types of realms. In theory and on paper, the majority of them were united into the Holy Roman Empire with Austria as the usually dominant Hapsburg leader. This was the political reality but the functional reality as experienced by the people was that of a fractured and divided Germany where economic growth was curtailed by local jealousies and international weakness. This unsettled life fostered discontent and a desire for more opportunity. These desires were exploited by the British and soon a torrent of German colonists headed across the Atlantic to swell the population of the British North American venture. The Germans had another benefit; they were by heritage enemies of the French and therefore could be counted on to side with their new government against their ancient enemy.

One major incentive that the British provided was the opportunity to become citizens of the Empire. All an immigrant had to do was live in the colonies for seven years, swear allegiance to the king, take communion in a Protestant church and pay a small fee and they became a citizen with the same rights and privileges of any natural-born Englishman. This process built a loyal population that within a generation became British in culture, custom and loyalty which combined with the increasing birth rate a larger population automatically provides soon led to the exponential growth of British North America. This growth in turn led to such a difference in size that by the time the final show down with France arrived, the ultimate victory was almost a foregone conclusion based upon demographics alone.

THE ATLANTIC AS A CONDUIT
FOR INFORMATION

No longer a barrier, the Atlantic became a well-travelled and well-known conduit for trade, immigration and information. Initially the colonies had been further away in time from Britain than the International Space Station is from Houston. Once the colonists arrived in the New World they were effectively cut off from European news and information dependent upon the occasional ship and if they were in the back country perhaps an itinerant merchant with news that was perhaps months if not years out of date.

As the colonies grew and as the Atlantic passage became a well-traveled road, these conditions changed. Newspapers began to proliferate and people began to expect some form of regular contact between the New and the Old Worlds. This brought the colonists into much deeper affinity with the Empire. They no longer felt abandoned at the edge of a howling wilderness they instead began to see themselves as citizens of a powerful and expanding power. While the largest newspapers were all found in coastal cities there were also several in the interior. All of these helped to integrate the colonies as they were shared and read by one person after another. These multiple news sources didn't dwell on local news they sought instead to have broader appeal hoping for the hand-to-hand currency that would garner a broad support and a growing reputation. Therefore they used their locations either on the coast or at some other hub of communication to re-print news from Europe in general and England in particular. What this accomplished was a diminishing of the natural impact of sectionalism or localism and an enhancement of the British character and Imperial outlook of the population.

THE ATLANTIC AS A CONDUIT FOR COMMERCE

What had once been an exclusively one-way trade, Homeland to colonies developed into a vigorous two-way trade and then into a multi-national trade that constantly grew. As the export of raw materials increased the colonials prospered and they began to desire much more than the bare necessities. The richer they became the more luxury items they demanded. The traders in Europe were only too glad to extend credit and although the volume of merchandise heading from America to Europe constantly grew it could not keep pace with the desire for the finer things in life. Consequently the upper echelons of colonial society found themselves in a debt spiral that for many kept them only one bad harvest away from ruin.

The increased economic activity highlighted one important thing; the average person in America was better off economically than the average person in Britain. They not only had a much greater opportunity to own property, but they also had a greater opportunity to rise in the social scale. In Britain, the society was highly stratified and the vast majority of people remained in the class to which they were born. Indeed, the hereditary nobility had a vested interest in maintaining such a tightly knit system of social control.

In the American colonies, many of the richest planters rose from nothing, often from being an indentured servant. Another contributing factor was that the colonies were virtually exempt from Imperial taxes. The tax burden in Britain was often crushing to pay for wars and the constant need to maintain a military establishment to protect and expand the empire. However, this colonial prosperity and social mobility was not universal. Especially in the cities there was inequality and often crushing poverty. In the winter when ice would close the Northern harbors and almost all trade would cease, there were particularly hard times for the urban poor. Of course poverty is always a relative term. The poor of the colonies were usually better off than the street dwellers and beggars of European cities. Even the tenant farmers who toiled from sun to sun for someone else and who often found themselves so hopelessly in debt to their patrons that it became a life-long sentence were better off than most of the peasants of Europe.

And there was also the frontier. Always off in the distance was the frontier, the ragged expansion horizon that constantly moved west. Here was a place where people could get a new start often with as little investment as an axe and some hard work a man and his family could carve a farm out of the forest and build a self-sufficient if not prosperous life. However, this was no panacea and no guaranteed pathway to success. Many people were unsuited to frontier life. Others shipwrecked on the shoals of resistance from those who got there first or from the indigenous people who stubbornly thought that their land was still their land.

THE EXPORT TRADE

As the Eighteenth Century matured the growing export sector became more and more important. The race for subsistence had been won in most places and the rich lands were being exploited in more productive ways. Tobacco, rice, indigo and timber products led the way. Many grew rich off the trade and they then sought for ways to enjoy that wealth. Following the lead of European elites the rich in Americas worked to build bigger and better houses furnished with fine china and staffed with liveried servants. Even on the frontier the successful wanted to display and enjoy their material success.

The relationship between the Homeland and the colonies was just as it was designed to be under the mercantilism which was their driving economic policy. The colonies furnished the Homeland with raw materials and then using the funds generated by the exportation of the raw materials purchased manufactured goods from the budding industrialists of the Homeland. It was a circular trade that kept all the funds within the Empire and contributed to the strength of Great Britain at every turn.

The prosperity of the great planters and the large farmers developed into a desire to live what they termed a genteel life, refined far beyond anything earlier generations of colonists could have imagined. The increased information provided by the colonial newspapers and the increased travel inspired and facilitated by the improving system of roads tended to homogenize and unite the upper echelons of society throughout the colonies and even with those of the Homeland. A sense of caste and class was born that was alien to the egalitarian milieu of the frontier.

One aspect of the large percentage of non-English immigrants that the Eighteenth Century brought to America was the development of a pluralistic society. All of the European societies that sought to colonize America were either to a lesser or greater extent xenophobic. They all saw themselves as the standard for development and society. None of them was especially partial to the culture of others and all of them lived in a world of them and us. If you weren't one of us, you must be one of them. The mixing of the English, the Scots, the Irish and the Germans combined with the leveling experience of the frontier produced a new type of society wherein people related to those with similar experiences instead of those with the same ancestry.

THE SLAVE CULTURE

The majority of those who came to America in the eighteenth century were not immigrants from Europe seeking freedom and opportunity. They were instead enslaved Africans kidnapped in West Africa by other Africans and sold into perpetual bondage. Over a million slaves were imported mainly by the British. This vast enterprise in human trafficking greatly enriched the British Empire, allowing them to surpass their rivals in the production of sugar and tobacco. There was an outlandish death rate that kept the African slaves from becoming an overwhelming majority even though in many areas they did become a majority. While millions were brought in, hundreds of thousands died from overwork and disease. The horror and violence necessitated by a slave culture degraded both the slave and the master.

There was quite a bit of difference between the culture of slavery as practiced in the northern colonies and the southern. In the north, there were no great plantations and no crops such as rice or tobacco which lent themselves well to slave gangs. Therefore, from the beginning the number of slaves in the north was much smaller than the number in the South. Whereas the slave holders of the South encouraged the slaves to wed and have children looking to grow their own crop of servants as opposed to buying them. The slave owners of the North discouraged this practice and in fact kept a much larger proportion of male slaves to female thus precluding any massive number of marriages among their slaves.

The African people in America in many subtle ways attempted to maintain their diverse cultural heritages but as time and contact with whites and other Africans from divergent cultures progressed; the African-American culture was born as a blend of all these influences. In the face of unspeakable and unconscionable brutality, they survived and eventually thrived in spite of all they had to endure.

★

REVIVAL!

In the middle of the eighteenth century, there were a series of great revivals which swept through the British colonies. Collectively they have become known as the First Great Awakening. This was a manifestation of the great Evangelical movement which was also sweeping the British Isles. Preachers thundered from hundreds of pulpits assuring people that Christ's millennial return was imminent and that they needed to get right before He came. This great wave of revivals also was marked by mass conversions of colonials, Indians and salves.

While it is a common belief that people came to America to find religious freedom in many cases that was neither the intent nor the experience. It should be remembered that the Europe of that time was preeminently a land of established churches. This had been a part of the peace formula that eventually ended the Thirty Years War. Each sovereign could choose his own brand of Christianity and then everyone in their country was expected to believe and practice the same way. Usually there was a state-supported church that everyone paid for with their taxes and which everyone was expected to attend. The church and state were so tightly united that to be a religious dissenter was considered the same as being a traitor to the realm.

It was from such a world that people came to America. Those who did come for religious freedom such as the Puritans did not come for religious toleration. Instead when they set up their colonies, they were as intolerant to others as the state church had been to them in England. Where religious toleration was practiced such as in Maryland or Pennsylvania, it was very much the exception as opposed to the rule. The whole idea of the separation of church and state was not only foreign to most eighteenth century Europeans; it was thought of as an aberrant idea which was detrimental to society and the general welfare.

Established churches fostered clergy who were dependent on government for their living and were thus usually compliant when it came to not preaching anything that could be considered as revolutionary or dangerous. Many of the churches even had lectionaries which proscribed not only what scriptures where read at what season but also what the topics of the sermons should be that accompanied those scriptures. To deviate was to invite retribution and often the loss of position. It was on the frontier that change was possible as the people themselves would often band together and build a church bringing in their own clergy who were then not dependent on the colonial government but instead governed by the congregational leaders.

In addition as the century progressed new religious ideas began to circulate. People began hearing of a God who was different than the dour, judgmental God of the Puritans or the lax accept-anything God of the Established churches. Instead they began hearing of a God who was rational, a God who loved and a God who was interested in the affairs of men.

REVIVALS

Revivals have always seemed to flow in waves, a brief intense period of activity followed by a trough of relatively quiet acceptance for the status quo. Revivals are usually sparked by preachers who are good speakers and by ideas which reach out and touch masses of people. Revivals spread by word of mouth and by the traveling of popular preachers to new locals. Revivals are usually emotional responses to emotional pleas. Often they are accompanied by physical manifestations such as the quaking of the Quaker revival.

In the frontier revivals of the eighteenth century in America, it was often the preaching of the doctrine of God's grace alone as being sufficient to bring a person to a personal experience of salvation as opposed to religious obligations or monetary giving. The frontier people could readily accept this and could then propose to change their way of life to match what they were taught God demanded of them, clean living and righteous behavior.

PREACHERS

Jonathan Edwards was one of the primary preachers who sparked the First Great Awakening. He was a second-generation preacher who had been brought up to be a minister and who took his avocation as a calling from God. He preached many famous sermons which left people emotionally responsive and ready to claim they had been changed forever: this wave of revival sparked by Edward's sermons swept throughout the North and moved fitfully along the frontier.

As this first great wave of revival seemed about to sputter to a close, another famous preacher arrived from England who was destined to have a lasting impact on American society and religion. In England George Whitfield was greatly influenced by reading a book written by Jonathan Edwards entitled A Faithful Narrative of a Surprising Work of God which was his account of the surge of revival which had so impacted the colonies. In this work, Edwards not only spoke of how this revival had moved from one area to another, he also described the style of preaching and service which had been the catalyst for the religious happenings. These styles were then replicated by many other preachers who saw varying degrees of response but whose emulation created a type of similar experience that was pointed to itself as a sure sign that this revival was from God.

The emotional and sensational (for the times) style that Whitfield developed in response to the reports from America put him at odds with the rationalistic and formulaic patterns of the established church. Whitfield was a dramatic and forceful speaker who was soon drawing immense crowds, crowds too large to fit in any churches so he began preaching in the streets and fields, anywhere he could draw a crowd.

In 1739 Whitfield crossed the Atlantic, becoming the first popular celebrity who was able to WOW the crowds on both sides of the Atlantic. He toured from Maine to Georgia speaking in churches and in fields and everywhere he went he created a sensation. He became fast friends with Ben Franklin who in turn used his publishing prowess to promote the English preacher. Franklin was a committed rationalist and didn't believe in Whitfield's type of emotional responsive religion but he considered Whitfield to be an exceptional entrepreneur and he appreciated his ability to promote himself. This was a mutually beneficial relationship. Whitfield allowed Franklin to republish his sermons which proved a successful means to increase the circulation of Franklin's newspaper. As a matter of fact the demand for Whitfield's sermons in printed form led to a massive increase in the number of pages printed in the next few years.

By the time Whitfield had returned to England in 1741, he had set in motion the religious revival collectively known as the Great Awakening. This was sustained after his departure by a multitude of preachers, many of them on the frontier. This religious revival had a positive effect on the customs and manners of the people. It also inspired many to learn to read so that they could study the Bible. This affected mainly the evangelicals such as the Baptists and the Methodists as opposed to the stricter Calvinists and the nominal Anglicans sweeping masses of new believers into the evangelical churches. The emotional preaching elicited emotional responses and many people were said to dance and sing, to wail and fall under the influence of the stridently emotional and evangelical preaching.

As the revival swept through the colonies, it became divisive. The evangelical preachers found themselves denied the pulpit in many established churches. Undeterred these itinerant preachers followed the example of Whitfield and instead began preaching in fields and street corners. In some cases these itinerant preachers began preaching against the established preachers who had locked them out. One is especially well remembered: Reverend Gilbert Tennent preached the sermon, "The Danger of an Unconverted Ministry." In this sermon Tennent indicted the established clergy as being unregenerate. He also said that in many cases they lacked a personal experience with Christ which he and other itinerant preachers said constituted the only credential which gave someone the qualification to preach.

These divisions solidified into what were called the New Lights and the Old Lights. The New Lights were the supporters of the revival movements and believers in the emotional personal experiential type of religion the revivalist preached. The Old Lights rejected the religion preached by the revivalist because it was not rational and too much based upon experience instead of tradition and received knowledge.

A further division was generated within the ranks of the New Lights themselves. This was between the Moderates and the Radicals. The Moderates accepted any minister or church that would accept the Revivalists and their message. The radicals went further than any of the primary preachers themselves stating that organized religion itself was corrupt. They extolled the emotional and physical responses found in the most intense revivals as the only true signs of the working of God. They went so far as to condemn not only the churches and the rationalistic preachers but also the government and any other man-made institution claiming that only those who had experienced the divine move of God as evidenced by the emotional and physical signs had any authority.

The radicals soon had the churches bubbling and boiling with controversy. Those who stayed with churches strove to convert these institutions into radical havens for the truly born-again. To do this they sought to expel any they perceived as being unconverted, including ministers. Where they constituted a minority, they agitated constantly for change. Where they constituted a majority, they pushed through their agenda. In many cases this led to church splits as one side cast the other side out. In many Congregational churches when the minority radicals were tossed out, they would join the Baptists who had been totally taken over by the Radicals.

IN THE SOUTH

The Great Awakening burned primarily in the New England and the Middle Colonies and along the frontier. It came belatedly to the South. It wasn't until after 1743 that the revival began to burn bright in Virginia and the Carolinas. In these areas it was the Baptists who carried the torch and set it to the dry chaff of the frontier. They moved swiftly and cheaply. A Baptist minister was typically not an educated or genteel person. They were instead often as common as the people they preached to having been just like them before they had themselves been revived. The Preachers not only moved and lived cheaply, something that couldn't be said about the established and the denominational preachers who required massive support, they also replicated themselves constantly. Many a town drunk heard the gospel according to the evangelical itinerant Baptist preachers, accepted Christ as their personal Savior and almost immediately began to preach themselves. These fast-moving easily replicated preachers spread the Baptist style and brand of Christianity far and wide across the South and it is still evident today, when a full 16% of all Christians in the South consider themselves some kind of Baptist.

The Great Awakening also brought a renewed interest in the conversion of slaves and Indians. Many were preached to and many came forward to accept Chris as their personal Savior. However, many were also shocked when the discrimination and prejudice that existed between them and the dominant society continued unchanged after their conversion.

As is always the case, soon the fire of revival began to dim. Beginning in the 1740s, the moderates among the New Lights preachers made peace with the Old Lights and they once again united with one denomination after another: they basically agreed to disagree about some matters but to refrain from denouncing each other or condemning each other as unbelievers. The Radicals primarily retreated into the Baptist fold while those among the Old Lights who could not abide any accommodation even with the moderates tended to retreat into the Anglican Church with its prayer book and strict liturgy.

★

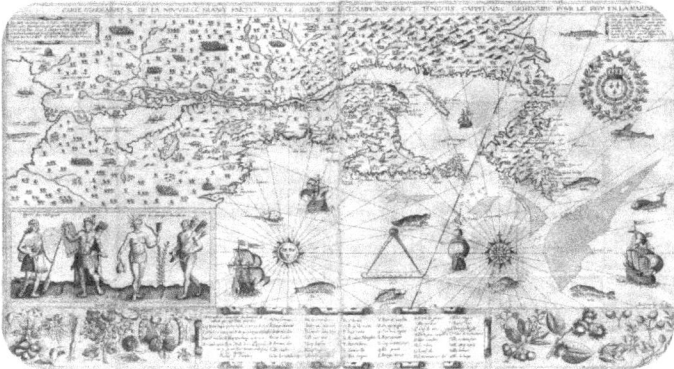

FROM QUEBEC TO NEW ORLEANS

For the French being weak in some ways made them strong in others. They had a colder climate and their rivers were ice bound for a good part of the year. This made them harder to attack. They had less people. This made their presence less onerous to the Indians and also caused them to seek better relations with the tribes building alliances which helped them have the manpower necessary to stand against the more numerous British. They had less economic activity and fewer settlements than the British. This helped them persuade the Indians that they were less of a threat than the constantly expanding British and facilitated them drawing Indians, even ones in British-claimed areas into their alliances. This situation applied to both New France (Canada) and Louisiana. In this way the French were able to effectively control a larger portion of North America than any other colonial power with very few people and a low expenditure of funds by the Homeland.

Contrary to their own cultural bias the French, who believed in a strict social hierarchy were forced by their relative weakness to treat the Indians as equals. They boasted of their power and the vastness of their possessions but in reality in most places the reign was in name only and a fiction on European maps. In reality the Indians remained sovereign in their possessions and the French were more of the officially accepted European presence in their respective areas. They would fight with and for the French when it suited their purposes. They would fight against the British because the British were seen as a power who sought to dispossess them from their lands and the French were only too glad to arm them in their fights with the British if not always join them in the battles.

After the British were able to take, hold and destroy the principle French settlement of Quebec in 1629, the French when they received their colony back in the resulting peace settlement set about expanding the number of inhabitants. They did this by pressuring the Company of New France, which was the monopolistic fur trading entity that had initiated the colony to begin with, to recruit more colonists. The French government had no direct control until 1663 when they took over the colony from the Company. The French, always sensitive to rank and privilege used a system whereby rich men were given titles of nobility (Seigneur) and huge grants of land for equipping ships and sending over colonists.

The colonists that France did send were mostly young single men who were without a means of support in France and thus susceptible to the offer of passage to America if it meant a regular supply of food. Few families immigrated and few single women. In addition, many of the young men who came as indentured servants or soldiers tended to return to France as soon as their term of service was completed. While the new recruits did swell the population when they arrived and while they remained, the constant flow of people back to France and the lack of women precluded the French from keeping pace with the rapidly multiplying British.

Much thought has gone into the question of why France, the most powerful, populous and expansive power in Europe during the seventeenth and eighteenth centuries was not able to overwhelm the rapid growth of the British colonies with numbers and material. This cannot be explained when we compare the available labor pools of the two countries. The peasants in France were even poorer than the peasants in the British Isles. Instead the difference might be found in the ties which still bound the peasants in France to the land. In England the enclosure movement had severed this tie for many and forced them into the cities where they eked out a wretched existence making them eager for any opportunity that might present itself. The French on the other hand while still poor, still hungry and still with little hope for an improvement were tied to the belief that owning their little farms was the only thing between them and utter destitution. So in the end it may have been the lack of an urban poor in great enough numbers that proved the undoing of the French colonial effort.

Another problem which hampered the development of New France was its location and its climate. Being so far north New France had a climate which was much harsher than that of France itself making it unappealing and also unsuited for the crops which had proven to be the economic lifeblood of American colonies, sugar, tobacco and rice. The few things that did flourish such as wheat and livestock were too bulky and hard to ship to make then profitable as exports. Even the fur trade, which had been the original economic impetus for the founding of the colony, was sporadic at best and since Britain was constantly shipping furs too, this was a trade with high competition and fluctuating returns.

And then there was the eternal war with the Five Nations. The French had stumbled into a perpetual war with the largest and best-organized confederation of Indian nations in North America. As allies of the Huron they had participated in several early attacks upon the unsuspecting Iroquois who were not yet used to European weapons or tactics. They had inflicted serious causalities on a people armed with only Stone Age weapons and in the bargain they had gained an implacable foe. The people of France had heard of the savage Iroquois and this knowledge did not do anything to help inspire people to volunteer to leave everything they had ever known to brave the cold for a new life in a New World.

LIFE IN NEW FRANCE

When compared to the lives they left behind in Europe those French who did make the journey and stayed in New France to become free Habitants found themselves in a much better situation then could have been expected looking at all the negatives previously mentioned. They typically lived on 100 acres of land they rented from one of the Seigneurs. This was much larger than any piece of land they could hope to control in France. They could hunt and fish as much as they wanted. In France this was reserved only for Nobles. They had diet built upon meat and bread both of which were always in short supply for the poor in France. Even their housing which was usually tight and warm thanks to the ready supply of building materials and fire wood was superior to what the typical poor person would expect in France.

GOVERNMENT

In the development of New France and the British North American colonies, we see a laboratory in the differences and the different result of a paternalistic, authoritarian, highly centralized command society competing against one based upon individual initiative, free enterprise and decentralized control.

The French had a highly centralized monarchy that believed in divine right. The King ruled with no interference from a parliament or council as King Louis XIV, who was king from 1661 to 1715 once said, "I am the State." The French were accustomed to following orders and suffering the consequences if they didn't. The French government was used to absolute control over the economy and the population and they expected their North American colonies to fit the mold and fulfill the vision of the king.

To begin with, the French instituted an awkward three-headed system of government meant to keep any one person from becoming too strong and which resulted in such internecine competition that there was more deadlock than there was administration. There was a Governor-General charged with over all command, an Intendant in charge of civil matters, and a catholic Bishop. Each had their own constituency at the royal court. Each had their own agenda. And each fought the other two for control.

There was no elected assembly as in the British colonies. Instead, there was a Sovereign Council appointed by the king and composed of five to seven Seigneurs in addition to the Governor-General, the Intendant and the Bishop. This council held all executive, legislative and judicial power. And this was a unitary power. There were no local governments in town, county or township as in the British colonies.

The military obligation was universal, all males between the ages of 16 and 60 were members of the militia and liable to call-up at any time. Everyone was enrolled in a company and every company had a captain. The captains served as local law and civil enforcement officers. Once again, as in all authoritarian states, fearing any one person gaining too much power these captains were always habitants instead of Seigneurs.

The strict stratification of France was translated to New France. There were more noblemen in New France than in all the more densely inhabited colonies of Britain and Spain combined. The great land grants given to the Seigneurs could not be sold or subdivided, ensuring that great estates would remain a part of the landscape and keep the habitants from actually becoming landowners. The Seigneurs were expected to live in the royal towns of Quebec and Montreal, maintaining a colonial version of a courtly society. And it was the Seigneurs who were given nearly every commission in the army, posts in the civil service and licensees to conduct the fur trade. This reinforced the class system and at the same time restricted the majority of the people and their talents from building a better and more prosperous society.

THE SECOND NEW FRANCE

In name there was one unified colony, New France; in reality there were two distinct areas each with their own situation. In the valley of the St. Lawrence River, the French followed the pattern of most colonies; they built settlements and the slowly spread out into the interior as their population grew. This is where the largest portion of the population settled and this is the area that is usually considered when discussions turn to New France in relation to the British colonies.

But this was only one section. Beyond the Great Lakes stretching west to the Mississippi and beyond was what the French called the Upper Country. This was a vast area that was the home of the fur trader. There were a few scattered settlements, small and completely dependent on the larger and more powerful Indian tribes who welcomed them and offered them protection.

There were a few forts, and a couple of towns however, by 1750 this vast area had only a population of approximately 2,000 while at the same time the population in the St. Lawrence valley had reached 52,000. The few towns and forts often acted as almost semi-independent districts. The distance from the royal authority weakened the hand of the king's representatives and the near proximity and power of the Indians often forced the local commanders to act in contravention to royal orders and in conformity to local realities.

The Iroquois had driven most of the French-allied tribes out of the east and many had fled their homelands finding refuge in great inter-tribal refugee camps west of Lake Michigan. They moved away from the shores of the Great Lakes to avoid the relentless pillaging and kidnappings of the Five Nations but they found that the further they retreated the further the Iroquois pursued. The only hope they and the French had was in unity against their mutual enemy.

Besides their monopoly on European manufactured goods, the French used another stratagem in their quest to penetrate the vast Upper Country and to tap its resources. More than their British contemporaries, the French married into the tribes. They would take an Indian wife, thus making themselves a member of a family and clan system. The new wife became an interpreter and teacher, a guide and a helpmate. These familial alliances were indispensable to the French colonial effort in the Upper Country and became a lasting feature in the area. Eventually the offspring of these numerous marriages formed their own villages and a distinct culture blending the native and the European ways.

In the rough country beyond the Great Lakes in many ways the French were the smallest and the weakest of the tribes. The refugees from the east and the indigenous peoples were all better suited to life in the woods than were the French. All had traditions and skills that stretched back thousands of years all adapted to living in the woods and off the land. The French by comparison were babes in the woods. They needed guides just to get around and instruction to do the simplest of tasks. How could they hope to claim suzerainty over the tribes or ownership over the land?

In native culture there was a long tradition, as in all chiefdom-type societies, of giving gifts to fulfill ceremonies and to seal bargains. The refugees had barely enough to survive and precious little to use as gifts and therefore, they could not fulfill the traditions. This is where the French wisely inserted themselves. They took it upon themselves to supply the grave goods needed for any who died. They supplied the trade goods necessary to facilitate truces and peace treaties between tribes, thus bringing order out of the chaos caused by the mass migration of the Iroquois' victims gaining for themselves a place among the tribes and the ability to claim the lands at least among other Europeans.

LOUISIANA

This area was first reached by French explorers led by La Salle following the Mississippi to its mouth. Upon realizing the vast extent of the Mississippi watershed and the strategic value of controlling a waterway that traversed the continent La Sale convinced the crown to establish a royal colony at the mouth of the great river. However, when he returned with a fleet of ships and colonists, he was unable to find the mouth of the river and established a colony some miles away in what is now

Texas. This proved to be a disaster that cost La Salle his life and the colony dissolved and returned to France. A later effort was more successful and a colony was established which fortified the mouth of the river and pushed inland attempting to link up with traders coming down the river from the Upper Country (Canada).

The French Louisiana colony never gained many inhabitants and of those that did come many were convicted criminals and slaves. As in the West Indies the slaves came to outnumber the free inhabitants. The French stood between the expanding British colonies of Carolina and Georgia and the Spanish to the west. They welcomed many colonists from the West Indies seeking a better opportunity than they could find in the overcrowded little islands.

Louisiana never developed a profitable export trade and was always a drain upon the royal treasury. The weakness of the colony and its situation between two other larger colonial powers pressed home the vulnerability of their situation upon the French. Consequently unlike the British colonies, Louisiana had a permanent military garrison which further reinforced the French authoritarian and centralized characteristics to the further detriment to the economic and social development of the colony.

As in New France, Louisiana was made up of two distinctly different areas. There was the plantation core which was analogous to the valley of the St. Lawrence River. Here the European settlers were occupying the land and reshaping it into a plantation system with slaves and expanding civilization. Then there was the vast interior which was only nominally controlled by France but which was in reality still Indian country.

The French treated any Indians they could as mere nuisances to be cleared from the land as they would trees. Further up the river as the relative strengths of the two parties changed, the French showed great deference for the culture and feelings of the Indians. In the ground in between there was trouble.

The Natchez Indians maintained substantial portions of the ancient Mississippian culture from which they had evolved. They had the ceremonial mounds, the intricately carved temples and the chiefdom style of government. The French felt secure enough to begin brow beating the Natchez acting as if they were a subject people even though they were still greatly outnumbered. In 1729 the Natchez staged a well-coordinated attack upon the French and they easily overwhelmed them. The French were only able to maintain their position by enlisting the traditional enemies of the Natchez the Choctaw and together they destroyed the Natchez.

After this rebellion, it was abundantly clear to French colonial authorities that the only way to maintain their security was through alliance with powerful Indian allies. From this point on, the policy of the French was to use the Indians as their militia one tribe against another and as auxiliaries against both the Spanish and the British.

CONCLUSION

All in all the French North American colonies were a disappointment to the crown. They never became self-sufficient. They were a constant drain upon the royal treasury. They became a cause of war and vulnerability during war. The French were never able to gain real possession of the land due to their small numbers and they were thus always held in the embrace of often unequal alliances with powerful tribes. Where the colonies of Britain and Spain enhanced the power of the home countries the French colonies were always detrimental and more of a source of pride than of strength.

★

THE AMERICAN STEPPES

The storied life of the Great Plains Indian nations is filled with contradictions. In the imagination of today it is easy to imagine the unsullied and pristine life of the nomadic Plains tribe, following the buffalo and secure in the vastness of their isolated terrain. Our mind's eye is shaped as much by Hollywood as by History if not more so. The reality is that without the influence of the white man the life of the Great Plains tribes, as we picture it, never would have existed at all. Their nomadic life was dependent upon the vast buffalo herds from which they derived every essential of life from clothes to food to fuel for their fires. Yet their ability to follow the herds and to efficiently hunt them depended upon the horse and the horse was introduced into North America by the Spaniards.

In addition the shifting alliances and power structures of the plains were influenced at their core as well as at their periphery by the exposure to European trade goods especially firearms. The tribes that could dominate the flow of European trade goods had an immense advantage over other tribes and the tribe that had firearms when others did not reigned supreme.

These shifting influences were impacted by European colonial policies and they in turn impacted the colonies. Take for example New Mexico. The Spanish cared little for New Mexico. It was poor and sparsely populated producing nothing of value and a constant drain upon their resources. However, it was seen as an important buffer zone between the warlike Indians to the north of their most prized possession, Mexico.

The British and French colonial efforts in North America grew from small infestations to the north of Spain's colossal empire eventually becoming colossal empires themselves. Spain declined from being the paramount power in Europe to being the sick man of Europe. And as these processes progressed, New Mexico gained in importance as the perceived need for a buffer grew not only between the Indians and Mexico but now also between the static Spanish Empire and the growing empires of Great Britain and France.

In Europe Spain and Britain were always rivals and that continued to be true in the Americas. However, in Europe Spain and France as the two major Catholic powers were generally allies but in America that did not always prove to be true.

The Spaniards relied upon the plains tribes to be enemies to be feared as far as the Pueblo tribes of New Mexico were concerned, thus causing the Pueblo peoples to remain the allies of Spain for their own benefit. But they also looked to their monopoly on firearms and horses to keep the plains tribes an enemy that they could easily defy. This situation was changed by the expanding networks of trade established by the French and the British.

The British had outflanked the northern French of Canada by establishing the Hudson Bay Company far to the north of the St. Lawrence Valley. Here they siphoned off furs and built a system of alliances that pushed ever southward into the Upper Country of Canada and into the northern plains claimed by both Spain and the French colony of Louisiana.

Into the Spaniard's settled pattern of enemies that could be defied who then inspired allies that could be controlled both the French and the British began to pump trade goods including firearms. The British impact was instrumental in encouraging the French to move further out into the plains to counteract their perceived threat than in actual goods reaching actual Indians. None-the-less the threat had its power and soon the French were visiting tribes all across the southern plains in an effort to gain allies before the British could penetrate the Great Plains from the North.

The Spaniards had been in contact with the plains tribes for more than a hundred years but they had little influence. The Spanish constantly attempted to impose their mission system and the plains tribes just as consistently rejected them. Then the French appeared offering trade goods with no missions. The French followed their pattern of marrying into the tribes and learning their culture as a means to gain influence as opposed to attempting to win the Indians over to the European ways. Not surprisingly the Indians preferred the French approach of gaining trade goods and keeping their own culture.

By combining the horse with the gun the many plains tribes cut themselves loose from settled villages and took up the life of nomads following the herds of buffalo, developing the iconic pan-Indian culture we are all familiar with today.

There were more than just the nomadic tribes on the plains. Along the larger rivers great horticultural societies that had existed for centuries continued to flourish even as the nomadic wave swept the area. These Indians such as the Mandan and the Pawnee were able to incorporate the horse, the gun and their settled life remaining powerful and secure even as the nomads grew and prospered.

New Mexico had been founded as a buffer for Mexico. Texas was founded as a buffer for New Mexico. The Spanish wanted to blunt the growing influence of the French and they attempted to do it by using their old tried-and-true method, expanding the border by pushing military outposts or presidios and missions outwards into the unknown. This was not as successful as they had hoped. The French offered guns for slaves and hides with no priests along for the ride. Armed with the French guns the plains tribes could attack the Spaniards and their missions sometimes even out gunning the Spaniards. As the Apache and Comanche tribes organized into efficient nomadic armies capable of clearing and holding territory, they pushed south into Texas. Their widespread attack on the previous inhabitants of the land caused the Spanish missions to grow as all the smaller tribes crowded in for protection. The Spanish population remained negligible and was barely able to hold on except in the major towns of San Antonio and a few smaller settlements and forts scattered about an immense territory. The only real growth came from the gradual Hispanization of the Indians at the missions.

THE LORDS OF THE
SOUTHERN PLAINS

The Apaches came first. They had been in the southern plains before they had horses. They consisted of many autonomous small bands living off subsistence levels as hunter-gatherers. They had fought and raided the settled Indians to the east and west. The Apaches had been the traditional enemies of the Pueblo peoples for centuries and of the horticultural villages along the rivers of the plains for just as long. They had mastered the skills and abilities necessary to survive and they had sustained themselves long enough to claim the title of the indigenous peoples of the southern plains. As they gained firearms and horses they became a more formidable enemy and a greater threat.

Into this mix came a new people, the Comanche. They were new-comers to the plains migrating down from the northwest. At first few in number they would soon become a torrent, overwhelming everyone and everything in the path. Once they had acquired guns and horses, they proved themselves to be the consummate mounted warriors.

The Comanche bands like the Apache were autonomous and jealous of their independence. However the Comanche had a much stronger affinity for group action than did the Apache. They tended to act together, many bands uniting to battle the Apache who were usually left to fight as one band at a time. In addition whereas most Indian cultures suffered from severe demographic decline during the eighteenth century, the Comanche actually experienced a tremendous growth until by the end of the century they actually outnumbered all the other tribes on the southern plains combined.

Because of the unrelenting pressure of the Comanche migration, the Apache were driven off the southern plains. Some moved to the northwest blending with the Pueblo people and eventually forming a new combined tribe known today as the Navajo. Others specifically the Lipan Apache, entered into the Spanish mission system at San Antonio while still others moved further south and west, becoming a perennial thorn in the side of the Spanish officials in Northern Mexico, and thus the Comanche became the Lords of the Southern Plains.

The Spanish finally awakened to their peril as these new realities on the southern plains caused their empire to contract. They had to admit to themselves that their mission system had failed to provide protection either for the mission Indians or for the colonies. Thus as the enlightenment thinking inspired a more rationalistic approach to governmental problems, the Spanish government came to rely more on stronger forts and stronger alliances. They succeeded in making peace with the Comanche in New Mexico and that strengthened that colony allowing it to grow in security but they failed to make the same peace in Texas. Subsequently the perennial war between growing Comanche territory and the contracting Spanish made the buffer colony of Texas marginal at best.

TO THE NORTH

The northern plains became the scene of the great rivalry between Britain and France which was to consume much of the eighteenth century. Here the French of the Upper Country sought to counter the influence of the British Hudson Bay Company.

The two powers followed very different methods in the North. France followed a policy of engaging the Indians, traveling with them marrying into the tribes and seeking to influence them from the inside. They embedded themselves in the villages and in the cultures. The British instead stayed at their outposts and expected the Indians to come to them for trade which they did.

Both tactics worked. Both produced abundant harvests of furs and both allowed the two rivals to claim vast areas of land that the really didn't occupy or control. The French tactic led to a greater understanding of the Indians and closer relations with more tribes but the British tactic cut costs, maximized effort and ultimately led to a larger and more profitable trade.

The French were convinced that they were almost across the continent and that just a little way further on they would find the Pacific and the long sought way to China. Because of this they continued to try and beat the British to the west following the trading paths with their various allies ever deeper into the northern plains.

Along the way they made the same type of mistake they had made in the east. Just as they had allowed an alliance with the Huron to drag them into perpetual war with the Five Nations, so they allowed their alliance with the Cree to lead them into a war of revenge with the Lakota. Their tactic of greater involvement in Indian affairs here proved to be a major weakness when compared to the strength gained by the British and their system of waiting for the Indians to come to them.

★

THE END OF THE FIRST
BRITISH EMPIRE

Britain and France fought a series of wars that raged around the globe in what were in all but name the first world wars. Fought for various reasons with different names they were all a contest to see who would be supreme as the preeminent power in Europe and as a consequence as the leading colonial power. These wars lasted with several breaks from 1689 to 1763 only to be renewed later on in the Napoleonic wars.

In North America there was a balance of power between the British and the French even though on paper it would seem as if the British should have been the insurmountable power. The British had a much larger population. Consequently they had a much larger colonial militia as well as the resources to support them. They also had a much larger and more profitable colonial colony to help bear the cost of both peaceful expansion and war. But despite these advantages France was able to maintain the fiction that they were serious rivals as colonial establishments and to also maintain the reality of the military ability to threaten the British Empire.

These series of wars worked to the advantage of the more powerful among the Indian nations. They played the balance of power game against the two rivals seeking the best deal at every turn. The Six Nation Iroquois Confederation (expanded from five to six with the addition of the Tuscarora in the early 1700s) were in a perfect position to do just this and though they had an ancient distrust of the French they were not above selling their neutrality if it could gain them an advantage.

The culmination of this series of imperial wars came about with the eruption of the Seven Years War in 1754. This war was not one either of the Empires designed or planned but instead one both of them fell into based upon their distrust of the other and their misinterpretation of the other's motives. A few false moves in North America in Nova Scotia and Ohio including the only surrender of George Washington at Fort Necessity followed by a major British defeat at the hands of the French and their Indian allies in the woods of Ohio and the war began.

At first the French were able to win a stunning series of victories due to their excellent use of their Indian allies and their superior knowledge of wilderness warfare. The British poured regular troops into the American colonies as never before. They sent battle-hardened veterans and excellent equipment pushing out from the seaboard ever deeper into the frontier.

Then after they had proved their worth over and over in the first victories of the war, the French Commanding General Montcalm let his disgust at the Indian's mode of warfare, including their torture of captives to lead him to rebuke them and attempt to set their captives free. This so enraged the Indians that many tribes refused to fight any more for the French. This also caused a major split among the French colonial command. Those officers who were themselves colonials understood the importance of the Indian allies to the defense of New France and those from Europe felt they could carry the burden alone.

Just as the allies followed a Germany first plan in World War II, so Britain followed an America first policy in the Seven Years War. With the buffer of the English Channel and the strength of their fleet to protect them from invasion, the British knew they could let the battles in Europe wait while they finished off the French in America where they believed they had the superior fleets and the overwhelming preponderance of resources on the ground. Following this policy, they continued to pour men and material into the battle for North America. Even when the war brought about a change in administrations they held doggedly to their strategy. At the same time they were able to effectively block the French from reinforcing their troops in the New World with an Atlantic blockade which was to become a feature of British warfare well into the twentieth century.

Finally in 1758 a powerful British fleet and army were able to capture the great French fortress of Louisburg which guarded the mouth of the St. Lawrence. With the way cleared, another fleet ascended the St. Lawrence River and besieged and conquered the hitherto impregnable fortress city of Quebec. This in turn led to a great campaign the next year with British forces converging on Montreal where they forced the Governor-General to surrender all of New France. The preponderance of British numbers and the ability to transport large armies and material over the Atlantic proved the undoing of the French. However their actual defeat was presaged for years by the continuing growth of the disparity between the populations of the two colonial ventures.

PEACE BUT NO PEACE

After the collapse of New France and the triumph of Britain as the hegemonic power in North America north of the Spanish Empire, it would have appeared as if peace would reign in the land.

There was however another circumstance which must be dealt with. Even before the ultimate fall of the French, the Indians began to realize that without two powers to play against each other they would be at the mercy of the remaining power. In fact even before the war was over, the British colonials began to act in a very high-handed manner towards some of the allies.

In Carolina the people began treating their old allies the Cherokees as a conquered people. They demanded the right to try Cherokees in white courts and they protected colonials who attacked Cherokees. When the Cherokees couldn't take any more, they fought back; however their Indian allies stood aloof, afraid to anger the now all-powerful British and soon they ran out of powder and shot forcing them to surrender.

Other tribes saw this as a portent of what would happen to them unless they found some way to unite and stand together. Several Indian prophets came forward preaching a pan-Indian self-awareness that caught the imagination of many as they realized they must hang together or hang separately. When this flared into spontaneous wars all along the frontier, the Europeans who could not comprehend such a group-think experience called it Pontiac's Rebellion, claiming it was a well-coordinated war led by one all mighty chief. It wasn't.

The war dragged on with terrible depredations on both sides. Eventually the Indians ran out of shot and powder and the British ran out of resolve, so they both made peace. The Indians continued to consider themselves independent nations and the British continued to consider them subjects of the crown. To mollify the Indians and in an attempt to avoid a recurrence of the war, the British tried to enforce a ban on colonial settlement west of the Appalachian Mountains, a ban they couldn't enforce but which caused great unrest among the colonials who looked upon movement to the west as a birthright.

THE END OF THE FIRST BRITISH EMPIRE

This set the stage for a great Imperial crisis. While the colonials greeted the fall of New France with jubilation, it soon led to new wars with the Indians. And while the British crown and government greeted the end of the wars with the Indians with relief, it soon led to war with the colonials.

The British Imperial government had expended great amounts of money to win the Seven Years War. They had sacrificed men and material like never before to protect and to expand the American colonies and as a result they had a dispirited and war-weary populace at home who were laboring under a crushing tax burden.

To alleviate this state of affairs the government looked to the colonies to pay their fair share but the colonies had grown and expanded under a policy known as benign neglect, wherein the Imperial government protected them and basically allowed them to do as they wished economically and politically. The colonial assemblies ruled as almost independent bodies assessing taxes and ordering their own affairs.

When the Imperial government began levying taxes directly, the colonials and their assemblies promptly complained and petitioned for a redress of grievances. The colonies refused to pay and the Imperial government sent tax collectors and customs agents. When the colonists attacked these agents of the crown, the government sent troops. When the colonials began to stockpile weapons and drill militia, the troops marched and so a brewing crisis in the colonies would spell the end of the first British Empire and the birth of the United States.

★

THE GREATEST OCEAN OF ALL

While the British and the French battled for hegemony in the woods of eastern America, another
series of adventures and struggles shaped America along
it Pacific coast.

Once again, it was more disinformation than
information which caused some things to happen.
The Spanish, ever wary of any threat to the jewel of
their empire, Mexico heard rumors of Russian settlers coming down the West coast and of British fur
traders tramping out of the wilds and they immediately thought of encirclement.

Russia had moved as Far East across the vastness of
Asia as the western European powers had moved west
across the Atlantic. They had built the largest empire
in the world by conquering one tribe after another until

they stood on the shores of the north Pacific. Then they took the jump across the short Bering Sea and landed in Alaska beginning their own colonization efforts.

It was a cold and barren land with few inhabitants but with a wealth of furs and fish. They soon established forts and trading posts and began to claim a large section of the northwest corner of the North American continent. The Russians came primarily seeking furs and built an empire in the north by exploiting the land and brutalizing the inhabitants. The history of Russian America was one of slow growth and slower assimilation. The Russians never seemed to befriend the Indians as the French had done, evangelize them like the Spanish or move them out of the way like the British; they merely seemed to impoverish and terrorize them.

NORTH TO CALIFORNIA

It was in response to the Russian boasts that they would move down the West coast to California that the Spanish after centuries of neglect finally began to colonize Alta California in earnest. They had claimed the area since the fifteenth century and they had outposts there almost as long but it was only in the eighteenth century that they began to apply the power needed to make their far-flung claims a reality.

The size and diversity of California is a wonder to behold. It stretches more than eleven hundred miles and includes more than a hundred million acres. Its climate rages from cool and foggy to alpine mountains to broiling desert to the lowest spot on earth. And before it was forever changed by the arrival of Europeans it had the greatest cultural diversity of any place in the Americas. Hundreds of distinct language groups and cultures fit into every niche in this vast landscape.

Into this world Spain intruded and proceeded to shape the land and the people to fit their view of what a colony should look like. The land was parceled out to grand lords who kept slaves and built dynasties. The mission system was set up and soon the wild diversity of the Indians was dissolving into the Hispanic sameness found throughout the Spanish Empire.

THE LAST PLACE ON EARTH

The Pacific Ocean was the last place on earth that the Europeans took as their own. It took many years of sailing this broad expanse to find all the many islands that had long been settled but had also long been isolated, including the continent of Australia and New Zealand. The French and the British were once again rivals as they sent expedition after expedition to find and exploit new lands. The most famous of the Pacific explorers was Captain Cook who would eventually give his life in his quest to find and explore these vast expanses of ocean.

The addition of the Europeans in the Pacific basin had the same effect it had in North America, cultures had to adapt to new realities and economies changed as new sources and new technologies were introduced. The eighteenth century saw Europeans reaching the most isolated islands (Hawaii) and finally learning that there was no Northwest Passage through the North American continent.

The great centuries of discovery had come to a close and the world which had been circumnavigated in the fifteenth century was by the eighteenth century being circled on a regular basis by European ships establishing and maintaining European Empires. And just as the cultures of the indigenous peoples encountered along the way had changed, so too the cultures of Europe had been indelibly changed by their contact with the rest of the world. The great Columbian Exchange had brought new foods to Europe which remain to this day mainstays of the population to this day. The gold and silver of the Americas changed the balance of power and fueled wars on land and on the seas for generations.

The colonies were planted by the Europeans, they grew until they were ready to stand on their own, then they did, from sea to shining sea.

★

RECAP, REVIEW AND CONCLUSION

CHAPTER ONE

From our politically correct, highly sensitized vantage point here in the twenty-first century, it is easy to say the prior presentations of American History was simplistic, or racist, or filled with gender bias, ethnic bias and Eurocentric. However, this critique could in itself be accused of being an exercise in Presentism, or the judgment of previous times through the distorting lens of the present. Instead we need to realize that every society must present a coherent story of why their independent and continued existence is justified and why it is important. Every society needs to teach their youth that there is a valid reason why the society must continue or it will soon break apart into its component parts. Multicultural societies will break apart along cultural lines, and multi-racial societies will fracture along racial lines, whatever the social tectonic plates are unless the members of that society are taught to believe in its relevance, it will become irrelevant and soon cease to matter.

However, when all the actors and all their stories are added in while the History may not be as consistently uplifting or as universally consistent, it is much more interesting and it is much closer to the facts. So keeping our eyes upon the past we have begun our study seeking an honest representation of our History as we seek guideposts that will help us navigate the future.

In the study we have embarked upon on, our goal is to journey between these two extremes. We will work to include all the voices while at the same time expressing the uniqueness of America, its History and its destiny.

First of all we must accept that the "wilderness" that has long been the stage for our understanding of European colonization in the Americas was not wilderness to the Native Americans to whom it was home. Many of these cultures had lived in the same areas for thousands of years. Others were newer arrivals. Whichever they were they had established nations and territories that were unmistakably developed and sovereign.

Second, the narrative cannot exclude the less savory side if it is to be in any way complete. Therefore in our text, we encountered the development of racially tinged philosophy, white solidarity and the oppression and exploitation of others that became an abiding feature of English colonization. The text also took notice of the fact that 50% of the population was excluded from political and social equality through the gender bias inherited from the past and transplanted to the new world.

In addition, the text attempted to portray a feature of American History which is often neglected or ignored; the proposition that in the colonial period there really wasn't an "America." The boundaries which we see as firm and fixed were then nonexistent. Each colony was a separate entity and unless they were surrounded by other colonies such as Delaware or Rhode Island, they all thought of themselves as having a growing frontier in the West. They all dealt with sovereign Indian nations as well as with the colonies of other nations. The Atlantic sea lanes were an open door to the commerce and navies of the world binding America and Americans in the growing triangle trade of the newly established European world community.

CHAPTER TWO

Several factors converged to create the climate for European dominance after the fifteenth century. The growing populations and limited resources provided a social impetus for expansion. The accumulation of wealth and a mercantilist economic policy which sought to make every country self-sufficient drove the Europeans to seek both raw materials and markets which could be appropriated as possessions. The development of technology in the spheres of ocean-going ships and weapons provided the transport and the ability to overcome the primitive weapons of what were almost always superior numbers of the indigenous peoples. A tradition of crusades, especially the Iberian Reconquista, and a feeling of cultural superiority combined with a religion based on evangelism provided a rationale for overseas conquest. In addition organizational skills and techniques in government, military and business provided the means to mobilize the forces necessary to confront and overcome much larger populations and the ability to impose their various colonial establishments.

The Spanish were eager to expand and exploit their discovery of the Americas. In less than a year Columbus returned with 17 ships and more than 1,000 men. The first farmers and artisans began remaking the islands into the colonial environment which was to become all too familiar. The introduction of slavery and disease soon decimated the native populations as the Spanish transformed the New World into an approximation of the Old World while the increase in the European food supply spurred by the introduction of American crops such as corn and potatoes increased the supply of potential colonists. When we combine all this with the detrimental impacts of the Columbian Exchange such as the introduction of pigs which soon became voracious wild animals destroying Native crops, the New World as an Eden ended as the Old World invaded.

CHAPTER THREE

The sixteenth century saw the rise of the world-girdling Spanish Empire, larger and more diverse than even the Roman Empire at its zenith, the Spanish Empire dominated the power politics of Europe. The steady stream of unemployed warriors Spain had to export conquered empires larger and richer than Spain itself in the Aztecs and the Inca. The plunder and wealth of the Americas fueled a lavish political and military agenda not to mention an imperial lifestyle for the proud Spaniards.

As time went on the other European powers began to see that while piracy could win immense profits it couldn't supply a steady income. In consequence, the drive to establish competing colonies was strengthened. Eventually Spain, which claimed all of North America, was face to face with strong and growing colonies by both England and France. Even some of the precious islands of the Caribbean, prized for their suitability to produce sugar were lost to the French, the British and even the Dutch.

CHAPTER FOUR

The Spanish explorers and conquistadors launched out into an almost frantic century of discovery. In a few short decades they had traveled the length of the Andes and marched north from Mexico to the Rockies. Founding missions on the ruins of conquered native villages they actively pursued a policy of replacing all the diverse native cultures with their own. The exploits of such notables as Cabeza de Vaca, Hernando de Soto and Francisco de Coronadot raveled further and saw more than any European since Marco Polo. They filled books with their stories and established Spain as one of the greatest patrons of discovery of all time.

In 1680 almost the entire population of 17,000 Pueblo Indians rose up and slaughtered every Spaniard they could find. Their leader Pope' told them that they could recover their former health and prosperity by destroying the churches and missions of the Christians.

The initial victory over the Spanish was tempered by the revival of ancient rivalries between the different Pueblo tribes. The Spanish regrouped in El Paso under Diego de Vargas and in 1691 were able to recapture New Mexico as far north as Santa Fe. Farther west, the Hopi and the Zuni were able to hold out and maintain their independence providing a safety valve for the re-conquered people of the Rio Grande valley.

CHAPTER FIVE

While the Spanish claimed all of North America their practical power did not extend far north of what is today the border between Florida and Georgia. In Europe the power of Spain forced the English and the French to diplomatically deny for some time that they were in fact seeking to found colonies in the Americas. The first colonies of both powers were strategically placed off the coast to avoid detection and destruction. As the sixteenth century progressed, the power of Spain waned as the power of England, France and the Netherlands expanded. By 1541 the King of Spain decided not to attempt to stop the French from founding a colony along the St. Lawrence which they considered far too cold and unpopulated to be worth the effort. This opened the flood gates and soon all these secondary powers began working to establish their own empires in North America.

The Jesuits followed the French as the religious order that made the strongest inroads among the Indians, especially the Huron. Many Huron villages became Christian as did large numbers of the people in other villages. This made for many disagreements and disputes among the tribe. Many wanted to retain their traditional beliefs and life-styles while others, seeing the power of the Europeans, wanted to adapt to the changing circumstances. This dissension led to aggressive actions on the part of the Five Nations. Seeing the opportunity to crush their ancient enemies and to obtain many captives they mounted sustained attacks, eventually leading to the complete destruction of the Huron nation.

CHAPTER SIX

Between the Spanish to the South and the French to the North the English sought to carve out their own colonies in what they called "Virginia" named for the virgin queen Elizabeth I. The English relied on private investors operating under royal permission to found colonies that were some of the first international joint stock companies. These promoters sought the quick riches of conquest and gold. But instead they found themselves in an area with a climate which initially proved deadly to Europeans and a land that had no easily obtainable minerals and that wouldn't grow the preferred money crop, sugar.

The colonists eventually grew in number and after the introduction of tobacco, they had a cash crop. Spreading out quickly within a generation, they were hundreds of miles into the interior, building forts and plantations. The freed indentured servants built new towns and constantly pushed deeper and deeper into the continent. When the Indians of Virginia had finally had enough it was too late. The wars against the Indians cost the lives of many colonists but they decimated the Indians. By the 1670s, there were more than 40,000 colonists and they were pushing the Indians back and out through the piedmont and into the foothills of the Blue Ridge Mountains.

CHAPTER SEVEN

While England was ruled by landed nobles and people of refined education and manners, Virginia and the colonies of the Chesapeake Bay area were ruled by merchants and mechanics that worked hard and made something of themselves in a new land. It was a meritocracy instead of an aristocracy. The rise and fall of tobacco prices spelled boom and bust for these colonies that depended upon the tobacco crop for almost all their cash.

The blight upon the Chesapeake colonies was the institution of chattel slavery first imposed upon Native Americans and then upon imported Africans. This system seemed to make sense to the planters because the Africans adapted to the climate better and could work harder. But it warped the realities of the economy and the society, creating a false sense of solidarity between the planters and the yeoman in opposition to the slaves. This stopped the yeoman from seeking to democratize the system and inculcated an inherent racism that became the bane of the area for generations.

CHAPTER EIGHT

Originally it was considered the northern part of Virginia and after a few unsuccessful attempts at colonization that froze and starved their way to failure it was considered an undesirable place to attempt a colony. Then, Captain John Smith of Jamestown fame made a voyage there and published a popular travelogue including a map and a new name, "New England" which enticed colonists into believing it was a fair approximation of Old England across the pond and it became an enduring success.

It may have faltered as a shining city on a hill and it certainly didn't create heaven on earth, but it was a successful model for a flourishing colony. Materially prosperous and politically independent, New England held out a promise that the New World could become something that really was new.

CHAPTER NINE

The Puritans didn't see the land they colonized as pristine, which it wasn't; and they didn't see it as merely undeveloped, which it wasn't, instead they saw it as a "hideous and desolate wilderness full of wild beasts and wild men." With such an outlook, is it any wonder that they looked upon the land as something to be conquered? Is it any wonder that they looked upon the Native Americans as inferior members of an inferior culture to be shunted aside at best and eliminated at worst?

In the wars that followed, the Mohawk Indians, one of the Five Nation Iroquois, allied themselves with the English seeing this as a perfect opportunity to smash their longtime rivals, the Algonquians. When the final war exploded in the quick victory of a surprise attack followed by the slower retribution of total defeat, the illusion of unity among the Indians soon began to crumble. The never-united tribes began to surrender one by one and their war to reclaim their land fizzled to a close when Metacom, the man immortalized as King Phillip, was killed by one of the Praying Town Indians in the service of the English. The Puritans cut off Metacom's head and mounted it on a pike at Plymouth as a warning to all who would dare resist their conquest of New England and thus died the hopes, dreams and memories of the proud Indian nations who had once owned the land.

CHAPTER TEN

The seventeenth century saw the rise of the West Indies to become the most important colonies of England. They were the most important because they produced abundant crops of sugar and sugar was what greased the financial wheels for the entire colonial enterprise. It afforded the profits and covered the losses to fuel a growing empire and the navy needed to make it happen.

In contrast to the wretched existence of the majority of the population which were slaves, the apex of society was held by the Great Planters. Growing sugar was an expensive proposition if it was going to pay. In other words, it takes money to make money. As time went on the land in the West Indies became more and more concentrated in the hands of a small minority of Great Planters who bought or muscled out the smaller ones. These Great Planters became fabulously wealthy and lived in a grand style in opulent homes surrounded by the finest imports from Europe.

CHAPTER ELEVEN

Unlike the other English colonies in North America the Carolinas were established under the auspices of the Lords Proprietors by West Indian planters. The

Lords Proprietors, eight extremely rich men, were based in London and they wanted experienced colonists to ensure the success of their financial venture. The Carolinas were unique not only in their parentage but also in their economics and their Indian policy, the infamous gun trade.

Georgia was founded by the Trustees headed by James Oglethorpe. As the only English colony to outlaw slavery Georgia was at the forefront of liberation and freedom in America but the experiment was not to last. Soon, planters from Carolina were migrating and establishing outposts in the territory. Within a short time the English colonists wanted to emulate the genteel society and thriving economy of Carolina. The Trustees tried to keep the lid on things by restricting the consumption of rum, and the avocation of lawyers among other things. However the great distance and the lack of understanding of the colonial experience on the part of the Trustees opened a wedge between them and their wards that grew greater and greater as time went on.

Eventually the divide escalated into open rebellion as the colonists sought liberty and property rights including the right to own larger holdings and slaves. Even before the twenty-one years expired, the Trustees capitulated to the rising demands and surrendered their rights and so Georgia reverted to the crown, becoming a virtual clone of Carolina.

CHAPTER TWELVE

Between the Chesapeake Colonies and New England there existed an expanse of coast and its associated hinterlands that would soon join the English holdings and become known collectively as the Middle Colonies. They had a better climate than New England and were healthier than the Chesapeake region. They proved extremely well suited for growing grains and raising cattle. They soon boasted a large and growing population.

The harmony of the colony was disrupted by sectional rivalries which plague the commonwealth to this day. The counties to the east are pitted against the counties to the west, each always striving for their own advantage. In colonial times this could deal with the perceived need for fortifications or roads, Indian relations or economic developments. The profitable colony of Pennsylvania could not keep pace with the lavish lifestyle of its proprietor and in 1707 William Penn found himself sentenced to an English debtor prison even though he personally owned a colony bigger than some European countries.

CHAPTER THIRTEEN

The always-grasping never satisfied Stuart dynasty had a rough time during their four reigns as the kings of England. They sought for absolute power and ended up losing the constitutionally power they had. The second one was beheaded by his own people and the last one was chased out of the country. The first and the third were wastrels who partied themselves to distraction and spent themselves into poverty. They are best remembered for the line applied to their restoration after the regicide and the Commonwealth of Oliver Cromwell: "They never learned anything and never forgot anything." All in all they were a sad interlude in a proud heritage.

Another feature of the eighteenth century British Empire was it suppression of the pirates which had once been an unofficial arm of its own foreign policy against the Spanish. As the Spanish Empire declined and the

British became the dominant sea power, the pirates had become more and more of a nuisance. Eventually the British used the same tactics which had always worked against pirates, sink their ships, burn their bases and hang those captured. This effectively suppressed the pirates and brought a measure of peace to the sea lanes so that a commercial empire like Britain could thrive. The British were preeminently an empire of shopkeepers and merchants. These middleclass entrepreneurs may not have had raw political power but they held economic power that could sway the powers that be.

The British colonies had been founded as economic enterprises and even after most of them devolved or evolved into royal colonies, they remained primarily an economic enterprise. Ever uppermost in the mind of the royal government, dominated by the theories of mercantilism was how can the colonies benefit the homeland? How can they contribute to the power of the crown? And while the empire of the English now spread around the world, it was profoundly an Atlantic worldview that predominated the thinking of the empire builders just as it was a European worldview that had predominated the mind of King William allowing the colonies to further develop as independent-minded enclaves in the midst of a far-flung empire.

CHAPTER FOURTEEN

That the Atlantic Ocean was a barrier between the Old World and the New World was attested to by the thousands of years the Americas lay in splendid isolation. Sporadic contact by the Norse, Irish fisherman and the stray mariner blown off course did nothing to end the nearly insurmountable barrier. Then, as the technological expertise of the Europeans advanced, as their navigation skills developed, a crack was made in the wall by Columbus. He was soon followed by larger and larger Spanish expeditions in the middle latitudes and Portuguese in the south. Soon their empires rivaled Rome and shifted the balance of power in Europe in favor of the Iberians.

The African people in America, unwilling immigrants though they may have been in many subtle ways, attempted to maintain their diverse cultural heritages but as time and contact with whites and other Africans from divergent cultures progressed the African-American culture was born as a blend of all these influences. In the face of unspeakable and unconscionable brutality, they survived and eventually thrived in spite of all they had to endure.

CHAPTER FIFTEEN

In the middle of the eighteenth century, there were a series of great revivals which swept through the British colonies. Collectively they have become known as the First Great Awakening. This was a manifestation of the great Evangelical movement which was also sweeping the British Isles. Preachers thundered from hundreds of pulpits assuring people that Christ's millennial return was imminent and that they needed to get right before He came. This great wave of revivals also was marked by mass conversions of colonials, Indians and slaves.

As is always the case, soon the fire of revival began to dim. Beginning in the 1740s, the moderates among the New Lights preachers made peace with the Old Lights and they once again united with one denomination after another; they basically agreed to disagree about some matters but to refrain from denouncing each other or condemning each other as unbelievers. The radicals primarily retreated into the Baptist fold while those among the Old Lights who could not abide any accommodation even with the moderates tended to retreat into the Anglican Church with its prayer book and strict liturgy.

CHAPTER SIXTEEN

For the French, being weak in some ways made them strong in others. They had a colder climate and their rivers were ice bound for a good part of the year. This made them harder to attack. They had less people. This made their presence less onerous to the Indians and also caused them to seek better relations with the tribes building alliances which helped them have the manpower necessary to stand against the more numerous British. They had less economic activity and fewer settlements than the British. This helped them persuade the Indians that they were less of a threat than the constantly expanding British and facilitated them drawing Indians, even ones in British-claimed areas into their alliances. This situation applied to both New France (Canada) and Louisiana. In this way the French were able to effectively control a larger portion of North America than any other colonial power with very few people and a low expenditure of funds by the Homeland.

All in all the French North American colonies were a disappointment to the crown. They never became self-sufficient. They were a constant drain upon the royal treasury. They became a cause of war and a vulnerability during war. The French were never able to gain real possession of the land due to their small numbers and they were thus always held in the embrace of often unequal alliances with powerful tribes. Where the colonies of Britain and Spain enhanced the power of the home countries, the French colonies were always detrimental and more of source of pride than of strength.

CHAPTER SEVENTEEN

The storied life of the Great Plains Indian nations is filled with contradictions. In the imagination of today it is easy to imagine the unsullied and pristine life of the nomadic Plains tribe, following the buffalo and secure in the vastness of their isolated terrain. Our mind's eye is shaped as much by Hollywood as by History if not more so. The reality is that without the influence of the white man the life of the Great Plains tribes never would have existed at all. Their nomadic life was dependent upon the vast buffalo herds from which they derived every essential of life, from clothes to food to fuel for their fires. Yet their ability to follow the herds and to efficiently hunt them depended upon the horse and the horse was introduced into North America by the Spaniards.

The French were convinced that they were almost across the continent and that just a little way further on they would find the Pacific and the long sought way to China. Because of this they continued to try and beat the British to the west following the trading paths with their various allies ever deeper into the northern plains.

Along the way they made the same type of mistake they had made in the east. Just as they had allowed an alliance with the Huron to drag them into perpetual war with the Five Nations so they allowed their alliance with the Cree to lead them into a war of revenge with the Lakota. Their tactic of greater involvement in Indian affairs here proved to be a major weakness when compared to the strength gained by the British and their system of waiting for the Indians to come to them.

CHAPTER EIGHTEEN

Britain and France fought a series of wars that raged around the globe in what were in all but name the first world wars. Fought for various reasons with different names they were all a contest to see who would be supreme as the preeminent power in Europe and as a consequence as the leading colonial power. These wars lasted with several breaks from 1689 to 1763 only to be renewed later on in the Napoleonic wars.

When the British Imperial government began levying taxes directly, the colonials and their assemblies promptly complained and petitioned for a redress of grievances. When they refused to pay, the Imperial government sent tax collectors and customs agents. When they attacked these agents of the crown, the government sent troops. When the colonials began to stockpile weapons and drill militia the troops marched and so a brewing crisis in the colonies would spell the end of the first British Empire.

CHAPTER NINETEEN

While the British and the French battled for hegemony in the woods of Eastern America, another series of adventures and struggles shaped America along the Pacific Rim.

The great centuries of discovery had come to a close and the world which had been circumnavigated in the fifteenth century was by the eighteenth century being circled on a regular basis by European ships, establishing and maintaining European Empires. And just as the cultures of the indigenous peoples encountered along the way had changed by their contact with Europeans so too the cultures of Europe had been indelibly changed by their contact with the rest of the world. The great Columbian Exchange had brought new crops to Europe many of which remain a mainstay of the population to this day. The gold and silver of the Americas changed the balance of power and fueled wars on land and on the seas for generations.

CONCLUSION

The story of the colonization of America is our story. It is the story of our birth and the story of how we set upon the road that made a disparate amalgamation of peoples from the four corners of the world into one Nation under God, indivisible, with liberty and justice for all.

Many different actors from many different places played their part. There was heroic bravery, insidious cruelty and everything in between. In this study I have tried to avoid the pitfalls of Presentism, the judgment of previous times through the distorting lens of the present.

I have worked to show a clear portrait of America's colonial past including the good the bad and the ugly.

This was from the beginning meant to be a History for the non-Historian. I have purposefully eliminated the footnotes and sources which are the mainstay of a traditional History book. I did this for two reasons:

1. To make it reader friendly for the non-Historian who isn't accustomed to or comfortable with the often copious notes which litter the pages of more scholarly tomes.

2. To inspire any non-Historian who finds something of interest in these pages to do the research themselves so that they can discover the joys of the Historical Detective discovering the trail of knowledge.

I pray that this has been an enjoyable journey and one that we may someday take to another destination as we sail the sea of time towards the horizon of understanding.

-Robert R. Owens

★

www.ingramcontent.com/pod-product-compliance
Lightning Source LLC
Chambersburg PA
CBHW030106070426
42448CB00037B/984